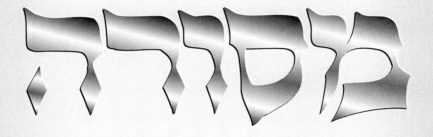

ArtScroll® Youth Series

Rabbi Nosson Scherman / Rabbi Meir Zlotowitz

General Editors

Published by

ArtScroll®
Mesorah Publications, ltd

A GADOL in OUR TIME

Stories about

RAV CHAIM KANIEVSKY

Adapted and translated by
Libby Lazewnik
from the Hebrew *Gadol Bekirbeich*

FIRST EDITION
First Impression ... February 2017

Distributed in Europe by
LEHMANNS
Unit E, Viking Business Park
Rolling Mill Road
Jarow, Tyne & Wear, NE32 3DP
England

Distributed in Australia and New Zealand
by **GOLDS WORLDS OF JUDAICA**
3-13 William Street
Balaclava, Melbourne 3183
Victoria, Australia

Distributed in Israel by
SIFRIATI / A. GITLER — BOOKS
POB 2351
Bnei Brak 51122, Israel
03-579-8187

Distributed in South Africa by
KOLLEL BOOKSHOP
Northfield Centre,
17 Northfield Avenue
Glenhazel 2192, Johannesburg, South Africa

THE ARTSCROLL® YOUTH SERIES
A GADOL IN OUR TIME — RAV CHAIM KANIEVSKY
© *Copyright 2017, by* MESORAH PUBLICATIONS, Ltd.
4401 Second Avenue / Brooklyn, N.Y. 11232 / (718) 921-9000 / www.artscroll.com

ISBN 10: 1-4226-1868-4 / ISBN 13: 978-1-4226-1868-4
Typography by CompuScribe at ArtScroll Studios, Ltd.
Printed in the United States of America
Bound by Sefercraft, Quality Bookbinders, Ltd., Brooklyn N.Y. 11232

∽§ Table of Contents

CREDITS:

R' Yitzchok Goldshtoff   R' Yisroel Kravetz
R' Refael Halevi   Kupat Ha'ir Archive
R' Gedaliah Honigsberg   Rabbi Eliyahu Mann
R' Yaakov Yisroel Kanievsky   Sefer Sho'ef Zorei'ach
R' Yanon Kashevitz   Shotafim L'Torah Archive

CHAPTER 1
Growing Up With the Steipler

The little boy gazed at the tumult around him. He was on a ship wending its way to Eretz Yisrael together with his family. They were surrounded by a throng of fellow passengers who spoke a babble of foreign tongues.

His father sat beside his young son, oblivious to everything

The Torah of Eretz Yisrael

that was going on around them as the two immersed themselves in learning. The other passengers looked in astonishment at the Steipler Gaon — R' Yaakov Yisrael Kanievsky — and his young son, Chaim, so deeply absorbed in learning Torah. A *Chumash Shemos* was open in front of them, and they were making progress. They were drawing close to the shores of Eretz Yisrael, and close to the end of the

Devoted father
and son:
The Steipler Gaon
and Rav Chaim

Chumash as well. In just a little while they would finish *Parashas Pekudei*. But at that very moment, the father gave the *Chumash* a kiss and ended their session.

"Let's leave a bit of our learning for Eretz Yisrael," he explained to his son. "That way, we will have the merit of making the *siyum* in the Holy Land."

In this way, the Steipler Gaon — one of the foremost *tzaddikim* in the generation — implanted in his little boy's heart the importance of Eretz Yisrael, mingled with the preciousness of Torah: the idea that the most important thing that we have in our Holy Land is our Torah learning.

All for the Berachah

Rosh Chodesh Nissan, 5694 (1934). A ship was nearing the port city of Haifa, bearing its precious cargo: the illustrious Kanievsky family. In just a few minutes the ship would weigh anchor in the harbor and the Steipler Gaon, who had already lit up the world with his Torah, would add his own holiness to the land's.

R' Mattisyahu Shtigel, the *rosh yeshivah* of Yeshivas Beis Yosef (Novaradok) in Bnei Brak, sent R' Tzvi Kagan — then a student in the yeshivah — to meet the Kanievskys at the port in Haifa and bring them food.

One of the foods that he brought for the newly arrived family were peanuts. Peanuts do not grow in Russia, from where the Kanievskys had come. They had no idea what it was or what *berachah* had to be made on it.

R' Chaim Kanievsky, then nearing his 6th birthday, peered along with the others at this unfamiliar fruit that had been sent to them. Usually, when small children encounter a new food, they immediately ask if they can have some, especially if they have just ended a long journey and are tired and hungry.

Though so young in years, R' Chaim looked at the unfamiliar peanuts and said, "Look, here's something we can make a *shehecheyanu* on for Pesach!" The child was not aware that peanuts are *kitniyos*. He merely saw in the gift of food a means to enable them to make the *berachah* of *shehecheyanu*, not food to make them full, or something tasty to enjoy.

His innocent remark, coupled with his happy face at this opportunity to make a *shehecheyanu* on Pesach, revealed a glimmer of his exalted character, a character that, even then, showed sparks of greatness.

R' Chaim Kanievsky grew up in a home of Torah. A home whose very air was filled with love of Torah and *yiras Shamayim*. His father

Memories From Kosovo was the Steipler Gaon, and his uncle was R' Avraham Yeshayah Karelitz — the Chazon Ish — each, one of the *gedolei hador*. His grandfather, R' Shmaryahu Karelitz, was a *rav* in Kosovo. R' Chaim's mother — the *rav's* daughter and the Chazon Ish's sister — used to speak of Kosovo's

Love of Torah

spiritual treasures. Later, R' Chaim told these stories over in his mother's name. Memories from the days when her father — his grandfather — served as a *rav* in Kosovo.

On the day after Purim, Kosovo would wear a solemn air. A group of about twenty youths would gather to learn a tractate of Gemara together.

These were *bechorim*, firstborn sons, and they had to complete the tractate by *erev Pesach*. If they finished the *masechta*, they could make a *siyum* and be exempt from the fast of the firstborns.

This was learning that knew no compromise. Learning that brought people together with a serious schedule and a clear goal of learning one *daf* each day.

"It seems," R' Chaim would add, "that the tractate that was learned was *Maseches Megillah*, which has thirty-one pages. It's the most suitable tractate to be learned over the course of a month's time."

R' Chaim Kanievsky's grandfather, the *rav* of Kosovo, saw the wonderful impact of such a regular schedule of learning, which renewed itself each year between Purim and Pesach. And he would say, "Too bad we don't have to make a *siyum* every month!"

The Steipler Gaon

Two Families in One Place

Rosh Chodesh Nissan, 1934. R' Yaakov Yisrael Kanievsky — the Steipler Gaon — and his family had left Poland and moved to Eretz Yisrael.

Where would they live? There weren't many choices. With no other option, the family settled into a cramped apartment.

Because conditions in the country were poor, they had to share the tiny apartment with another family. Only a thin wall made of wood divided the single apartment in two. There was very little privacy. Conversations were easily overheard on both sides of the partition.

This was not a situation that anyone would choose, even in those trying times. But, looking back, something positive came from the two families living side by side in that limited space.

The family who lived on the other side of the wooden divider had the merit of being close to the Kanievsky family. Hashem had given them the chance to learn from the family's behavior and outlook on life.

Before long, the father became a huge admirer of his holy neighbor and his family. The walls themselves told of the Steipler's diligence in learning and of his piety. They could speak of his righteousness and honesty, of his *yiras Shamayim,* and his love of *chesed* and fine *middos.* The walls saw how he much he loved Torah, which he studied day and night. All this the neighboring family heard and saw with their own ears and eyes.

As for the Steipler Gaon's family: they, too, benefited from their neighbors. The neighbor considered it his privilege to help support the Steipler with money and clothing. From time to time, he provided necessary help to his neighbor on the other side of the wall.

> *"You see? We can have such an influence on others without even saying a word,"* R' Chaim Kanievsky *later said when he talked about this time in his family's life. "This reminds me of the advice that the Vilna Gaon once gave to the Dubno Maggid."*
>
> *The Dubno Maggid asked the Vilna Gaon, "How can I succeed in influencing others?"*
>
> *The Vilna Gaon answered, "Our impact on our surroundings is like pouring wine. When a person pours wine into a full cup of wine that has smaller cups around it, the wine in the large cup will overflow to fill the smaller cups as well.*

"That's how it is with our effect on those who surround us. If we fill ourselves with yiras Shamayim, the overflow will erupt and influence the people around us in the most positive way!"

The Chazon Ish, who was recognized as the *gadol hador* in his time, was the brother of Rebbetzin Kanievsky, the Steipler's wife —

Who Knows Five? R' Chaim's mother. The Chazon Ish had come to Eretz Yisrael in the summer of 1933. He had been living there for nearly an entire year before the Kanievskys arrived.

The Kanievskys settled in Bnei Brak, close to where the Chazon Ish was living. At the time, R' Chaim Kanievsky was just 6 years old.

When he saw his uncle, the Chazon Ish, the little boy ran to him and cried, "Uncle, I made a *siyum* on *Chamishah Chumshei Torah!*"

Many years passed. The times changed, but the values — never.

One of R' Chaim's great-grandchildren came to his home to be tested on *Chumash Bereishis*. R' Chaim was very happy with his knowledge and parted warmly from him.

Later on, R' Chaim asked, "How old is the child?"

"Five and a half," came the answer.

"*Nu*," R' Chaim said, "it's not so amazing. He's a big boy already."

After all, at that age R' Chaim had already finished learning all five Books of the *Chumash*!

"I'm going to learn, *im yirtzeh Hashem.*"

"I'm going to the store, *im yirtzeh Hashem.*"

Spare Part This was the Steipler's custom: whenever someone told him about a future plan, he would add the words *im yirtzeh Hashem* — "if Hashem wills it."

One day, the Kanievskys' washing machine stopped working. The technician said that one of the machine's parts had broken, and they needed to buy a new spare part from a certain store in Tel Aviv.

R' Chaim's sister was sent to Tel Aviv to buy the needed part for the machine. She decided to use her time in Tel Aviv to take care of another matter.

"I'm going to Tel Aviv to buy a part for the washing machine," she told their father, the Steipler.

The Steipler added, "You should say, 'Im yirtzeh Hashem'!"

After an exhausting trip, R' Chaim's sister returned home. While she had manage to complete her other errand, she had not managed to buy the spare part for the washing machine.

From that day, R' Chaim and his sister paid attention to a small but very significant "spare part" that directly affects one's success and, when absent, seems to remove success. From then on, they undertook to say, "Im yirtzeh Hashem," regarding every future action, as their father did.

The Missing Plant

The Arab riding the horse turned to the Jewish boy and waved a hand as though to ask, "What do you want? Why did you just tug at my clothes?"

The boy told him the name of a certain plant that the Arabs used to make wicks for burning. "Can you show me that plant?" he asked.

Rav Chaim
lights the wicks

The Arab motioned for him to follow. He rode through the fields surrounding Bnei Brak until he found the plant.

"Here," he told the youth. "Here is the plant you are looking for."

Who was that young boy? Which plant was he seeking — and why?

The boy was R' Chaim Kanievsky. He had just learned the chapter in the Mishnah in *Shabbos* called *"BaMeh Madlikin."* This chapter outlines all the various types of wicks and oils that may be used for Shabbos lights. R' Chaim had a powerful desire to know each of the different kinds of wicks mentioned in the Mishnah. He took a small box and began collecting all the plants listed there.

He identified each of the plants with the guidance of his uncle, the Chazon Ish, and his father, the Steipler. Gradually, the box filled. Only one thing was missing from it: a plant that neither the Chazon Ish nor the Steipler succeeded in identifying.

They told R' Chaim that the Arabs knew which plant it was. The boy did not give up.

In those days, several Arab families lived in and around Bnei Brak. He decided to inquire about the plant from them.

When he returned home with the missing plant, he immediately added it to his box, along with the other wicks mentioned in the Mishnah. This unique collection remained with R' Chaim for many years, until someone — not realizing its worth — threw it in the trash.

When R' Chaim Kanievsky was a young boy, his parents lived near the Chazon Ish in Bnei Brak. The boy longed to learn *hilchos kilayim* (the laws of forbidden mixtures) very thoroughly.

A Living Torah

What did he do? He prepared the soil in the courtyard of his home and planted several kinds of vegetables. Now the laws of *kilayim* were visible before him. One of the halachos of *kilayim* is that different kinds of plants should not grow too close to each other so that they do not mix together. The young boy asked the Chazon Ish how much space must be maintained between one

R' Chaim still enjoys a garden

plant and the next. The Chazon Ish instructed him to leave a *tefach* and a half (almost 6 inches) between one variety and another.

In this way, the Torah came alive for R' Chaim, until he himself grew to become a *Toras chaim* — a living Torah!

R' Chaim was a young boy at the time. Both his father — the Steipler Gaon — and Chaim were running a fever. Both lay helplessly

Keeping Busy in the Sickbed
in bed. But for the Steipler, this was not a reason to take a break from learning Torah.

The Steipler found a *sefer* that was suitable for a boy his son Chaim's age, the condition of his health, and his own illness.

Chaim lay in bed, holding a volume that contained sayings and aphorisms. Beside him, two other books waited their turn. All three volumes were compiled from sayings found in the Talmud, the Midrash, and various other sources.

"You read the sayings," the Steipler told Chaim, "and I'll have to tell you where they are found."

They began. Chaim read the first saying, and his father instantly responded with the source: "Gemara *Shabbos*," and he named the exact *daf* and *amud*. The next quote was from *Kiddushin*, and the third from *Gittin*...

Chaim was able to check his father's answers because each saying had the source written next to it. He was stunned. One might have thought that his father was holding the book instead of him! The Steipler didn't miss one source, whether it was from a tractate of Gemara, from *Midrash Rabbah* or *Midrash Tanchuma*, or some other source.

Here and there, the Steipler would pause. "This one," he said thoughtfully, after Chaim read a saying whose source he could not place, "I don't know. It must be from the *Zohar*."

The Steipler was correct about that, too. That saying did have its source in the *Zohar*.

Chaim continued to read aloud, saying after saying, page after page, one book after another. The Steipler, who was still a young man then, gave the sources quickly and accurately, except for the occasional, "I don't know that one — it must be from the *Zohar*." And even those answers were incredibly correct!

It was a challenging pastime, and an amusing one for a sick child. But when R' Chaim grew up, he was left with a powerful memory that remained with him forever. A memory that shows him, to this day, what can be accomplished through hard work.

When R' Chaim was 12 years old, he had a daily session with his father to learn *Perek Kol Sha'ah* in Gemara *Pesachim*. His uncle, the Chazon Ish, would sit nearby and listen to them

Growing Up learning, occasionally inserting a comment of his own. By the time they were done, the clever young boy was able to discuss that *perek* in depth with great Torah scholars.

R' Chaim had the privilege of learning many tractates of the Gemara with his father before he became a bar mitzvah, including difficult ones such as *Eiruvin*, *Zevachim*, *Menachos*, and *Chullin*.

Before they began *Maseches Chullin*, a particularly difficult trac-tate, R' Chaim accompanied the Steipler to a slaughterhouse. There he was shown how animals were *shechted,* so that learning the *masechta* on slaughtering would be more easily understood.

But they didn't learn the entire *Shas* together. The Steipler instructed his son to learn a portion of the Gemara on his own. Between the *masechtas* he learned with his father and those he learned on his own, R' Chaim completed all of *Shas* with *Tosafos* by the time he was 16.

When R' Chaim became a father himself, he did as his own father had done and learned *Shas* with his sons (without *Tosafos*) even before they were bar mitzvah. He would relate that the tractates he learned when he was younger were clearer to him to this day than the ones he learned later, close to the age of 16. He learned *Maseches Bava Kamma* last of all, and to this day it is less clear to him than any of the others.

"That," R' Chaim declared, "is the power of '*girsa d'yankusa*' — knowledge acquired in childhood!"

Apart from learning with his father, as a child R' Chaim was offered the continual opportunity of talking in Torah with his uncle, the Chazon Ish.

When he was learning *Maseches Eiruvin* with his father, R' Chaim asked the Chazon Ish, "How it is possible to make both an *eiruv chatzeiros* and an *eiruv techumin*? Where is the person's home — here in his courtyard, where he made his *eiruv chatzeiros,* or wher-ever he placed the *eiruv techumin*?"

"Good question!" the Chazon Ish said with approval.

In this way, R' Chaim grew up with his uncle's encouragement. When he would tell this story, he would add, "The question I asked that day is not really a question at all, since both of those things are *tik-kunim* by Chazal." That means that Chazal apply whatever conditions they deem appropriate according to the situation. Still, even though it wasn't really a question, the Chazon Ish praised him, encouraging him to continue to ask questions in his learning.

The Steipler at a bar mitzvah

R' Chaim's bar mitzvah took place in Yeshivas Beis Yosef in Bnei Brak. In its honor, they served cake and wine. The Chazon Ish came,

An Old-Time Bar Mitzvah as well as the *rav* of Ponevezh and some friends from the Talmud Torah, the elementary school that R' Chaim attended.

The Kanievskys' neighbor prepared a few invitations using his typewriter. R' Chaim delivered a *derashah* on *"hesech da'as b'tefillin"* — a lapse of attention when wearing *tefillin* — and branched out into the laws of *tumah* in connection with the *korban Pesach*.

The *derashah* was subsequently printed in one of his father's *sefarim*, which contain *chiddushim* in Torah.

R' Chaim said the entire *derashah*, and no one interrupted him! And presents?

There were presents, too. R' Chaim received seven *sefarim* and several were from his uncle, the Chazon Ish. He received the *sefer Chazon Ish* on *Eiruvin*, a *Mesillas Yesharim*, and R' Yehoshua Karelitz, a relative, brought a set of *Mishnayos*.

A few typed invitations, wine, cake, seven presents, two *talmidei chachamim*, and his classmates. That was the sum total of a bar mitzvah in those far-off days.

R' Chaim at
his father's *kever*

A lifelong love
of *sefarim*

R' Chaim's sister once related to him that one time their father,
the Steipler Gaon, felt ill and went to sleep. She told her father to

**Two Different
Mitzvos**
wake her up if he didn't feel well and needed her.
In the morning, he told her that he'd felt very
unwell during the night.

"Then why didn't you wake me up?" his daughter asked.

"You have a mitzvah of *kibbud av va'eim*," the Steipler said, "and
I have the mitzvah of not bothering you."

When R' Chaim's *sefer Sha'arei Emunah* on *Maseches Pe'ah* was
published in 2002, one of his *shamashim*, R' Eliyahu Mann, asked the

**A Special
Interest**
gadol whether he had always had a special interest in
Seder Zera'im. This section of Mishnah covers *terumos*
and *ma'asros*, and other similar subjects.

"Actually, yes," R' Chaim responded. "Before I was bar mitzvah,
my father, the Steipler, learned all six *Sidrei Mishnah* with me twice,

because *Mishnayos* includes the entire Torah. As a *bachur*, I learned *Zera'im* with the commentary of the Rosh and saw that it needed explanation. Even then, I entertained the idea of writing an additional explanation of my own."

Summer vacation. The Kanievsky family had taken a vacation in Tzefas during *bein hazemanim* together with the Chazon Ish.

In the Shade of Giants

R' Chaim was learning *Maseches Ta'anis* at the time, and he asked his uncle to learn with him. Over the course of the days they spent in Tzefas, R' Chaim learned *Maseches Ta'anis* together with the Chazon Ish. When R' Chaim grew older, he wrote many *sefarim*. When he produced the third volume of his *sefer, Siach HaSadeh*, which deals with *Maseches Ta'anis*, he set down some of the original Torah thoughts that he'd had in his youth while learning with the Chazon Ish in Tzefas.

"In every *sugya* in *Shas*," R' Chaim would say, "I can tell you what the Chazon Ish would have asked on the topic."

"And what about the answer?" someone would ask.

"If I knew what the Chazon Ish would have answered on every *sugya*," R' Chaim responded, "then I could have written the Chazon Ish's *sefarim* myself!"

The Chazon Ish

It was during the *shivah* for R' Yaakov Shneidman, *zt"l*, who

Rav Chaim's "Game"

had been *rosh yeshivah* of Tiferes Tzion. The yeshivah for high-school-age boys had been founded by the Chazon Ish along with R' Yaakov, and R' Chaim had been one of its first students.

An elderly Jew entered the house to comfort the mourners. He brought up memories of the past. "In my youth, I learned in Yeshivas Tiferes Tzion," he said. "Rav Chaim Kanievsky, *shlita*, learned there with me.

"Even as a boy, he was different from the other boys. One of the differences between R' Chaim and the

A moment of quiet thought

other students was the way he used breaks. As young boys, we have breaks during the day to play and relax. R' Chaim found a way to 'amuse' himself during those times as well. How did he 'play'? His game was to count the number of times Abaye is quoted in the Gemara, how many times Rava appears, and so on."

CHAPTER 2
From the Lomza Yeshivah to Fatherhood

R' Chaim had graduated from Yeshivas Tiferes Tzion. He was now learning in the Lomza Yeshivah in Petach Tikvah. R' Chaim would return home for Shabbos. When Shabbos ended, his mother would send food with him to take back to the yeshivah. Upon arriving in

Care Package

yeshivah, R' Chaim would set the food down somewhere and then, absorbed in his learning, completely forget to eat it.

A solid week would go by, a week filled with learning. The food remained neglected. Finally, Friday came around — the day he was due to return home for Shabbos. It was then that he'd notice the package of food that his mother had packed for him to eat all week.

On the spot, he sat down and ate it all before returning home. That way, he could tell his mother that he'd eaten the food that she'd prepared for him.

A new week began, and with it a new package of food. Once again, the food sat and grew stale day by day. Only on Friday did the diligent *bachur* eat it all, just to make his mother happy.

And that was how it continued with his packages of food throughout the year.

Those who learned in Lomza Yeshivah in Petach Tikvah at the same time as R' Chaim Kanievsky remember how he spent every moment immersed in Torah.

Blackout in the Beis Midrash

One night, the *beis midrash* was very dark because of a power outage. The students were finding it hard to learn in the blackout.

One student got up and went to the window. If he couldn't concentrate on Gemara, he could use the time to learn the weekly *parashah* by the weak illumination of the streetlamps. Another got up and went over to a fellow student to talk to him in learning. Yet a third had some urgent business to attend to and figured that this was the best time to take care of it, and so on.

The *bachurim* of Lomza Yeshivah, survivors of the war in Europe, were serious and diligent students. They certainly tried not to waste the time. But when there were no lights, it was hard not to become distracted.

Only one of them behaved differently that night. When the lights went out, R' Chaim left the *beis midrash* for a moment, and then sat back down in his seat with a candle and some matches. Within seconds, his Gemara was open, and his regular learning continued without disturbance, as though nothing had happened!

It was afternoon in Lomza Yeshivah in Petach Tikvah. This was the hour when the *beis midrash* usually emptied out. The *bachurim* took an afternoon nap to recharge their batteries for additional hours of productive learning.

The Learning Never Stops

R' Chaim Kanievsky was a student at the yeshivah. He went to rest as well, but he pursued a different kind of rest. R' Marcus, who had the privilege of learning with R' Chaim in those long-ago days, relates what R' Chaim used to do: each afternoon, when everyone left to take a nap, R' Chaim would pick up a small Gemara, find a bench in the empty *beis midrash*, lie down, and learn. The other boys would joke that R' Chaim learned even when he was resting.

Always
learning

As time went on, this stopped being a joke. It became something that his family witnessed on a regular basis. Sometimes, when R' Chaim slept, the sounds of Torah learning would he heard from his room. His relatives would enter and listen in astonishment to the profound things he said while he slept.

The old saying — "He learns even when he's asleep" — turned out to be amazingly true in his case!

Young boys, and even older ones, can sometimes make the mistake of thinking that greatness is for people who were born that way.

Building Greatness, One Brick at a Time

But that's not true. Greatness is built one brick at a time: a process of constant, nonstop work from childhood until old age. Greatness in Torah is something that is acquired in the next minute, the next hour, the next month, and the next year.

R' Moshe Soloveitchik, *zt"l*, and, *l'havdil bein chaim l'chaim,* R' Chaim Kanievsky used to learn together in the Lomza Yeshivah in Petach Tikvah. They were also roommates for about half a year.

Rav Chaim and Rav Aharon Leib

R' Moshe, who already recognized R' Chaim's greatness, asked to room with him. As his roommate, R' Moshe had a golden opportunity to observe how precious the Torah was to R' Chaim.

During those six months, there were numerous occasions when one could witness R' Chaim's total dedication to Torah, every minute of his life. R' Moshe Soloveitchik sensed that he had the privilege of living with a *bachur* who was utterly devoted to Hashem and His Torah. The Torah was the joy of his life!

He shared his impressions of R' Chaim with his old friend from Brisk and Switzerland — R' Aharon Leib Shteinman. "You'll see," he told R' Shteinman in those long-ago days. "People are going to run after him to get *berachos*!"

R' Moshe and R' Chaim also learned *Maseches Temurah* together. When R' Moshe Soloveitchik married and left the yeshivah, they had not yet completed the *masechta*. "We'll finish it one day," R' Moshe consoled his *chavrusa*.

But many years passed, and *Maseches Temurah* was still waiting. They were years of toil in Torah, but not of joint labor. And then R' Moshe Soloveitchik died and left this world. What about *Maseches Temurah*?

R' Moshe had said that they would finish the *masechta*, but —

"Perhaps we will have the merit of finishing it after *techiyas hameisim*," R' Chaim said after R' Moshe's passing.

Though R' Moshe was not able to finish learning the tractate together with R' Chaim, nevertheless his vision came true. The boy he had learned and roomed with grew up to become a *gadol b'Yisrael* — someone to whom everyone came for *berachos*.

Those who visit that special house know that greatness is built one brick at a time. And it began with hour after hour of learning in front of a *shtender* in Lomza Yeshivah, in Petach Tikvah, eighty years ago!

During the *shivah* for R' Reuven Yosef Gershonowitz, *zt"l*, R' Yaakov Edelstein, the *rav* of Ramat HaSharon, related the following

Despite the Heat
story when he came to comfort the mourners:

When we were young *bachurim*, we learned together in Yeshivas Lomza in Petach Tikvah. R' Chaim Kanievsky was learning there at the same time.

Yeshivas Lomza

A very special bookcase

I remember once, it was a hot day. Given the humidity in Petach Tikvah, the weather was unbearable. The *bachurim* who couldn't stand the heat wanted to make it a little easier on themselves, so they rolled up their sleeves a bit.

Only two *bachurim* continued to learn as usual, with their sleeves covering their arms. They were R' Reuven Yosef Gershonowitz and — *l'havdil bein chaim l'chaim* — R' Chaim Kanievsky.

There was a practice in Yeshivas Lomza to give the *bachurim* half a lira each month. This money enabled them to pay for various expenses.

Give to a Wise Man

R' Chaim Kanievsky, who was attending the yeshivah then, received the same monthly sum. But his needs were met by his parents, so he used the money he saved up to buy *sefarim* from time to time. Ten years of learning in Yeshivas Lomza didn't satisfy his hunger for new *sifrei kodesh*. "Give to a wise man, and he will become wiser." Those monthly half-lirot, totaling six lirot a year, expanded his library greatly.

Later, when he married, his father, the Steipler, built a bookcase for all of his son's *sefarim* with his own hands. To this day, that bookcase stands on the north wall of the Kanievsky home.

When R' Chaim Kanievsky learned at Yeshivas Lomza, one of the *bachurim*, a student of his, got married in Jerusalem. R' Chaim did not attend the wedding.

Thirty Years Ago

"Why didn't you go to the wedding?" another of his students asked him.

"I have no time," R' Chaim apologized. Then he added, "*B'ezras Hashem*, when you get married, I'll go to your wedding, *bli neder*."

Later, that *bachur* transferred to a different yeshivah. Ten years passed. The *bachur* did not forget his rebbi, R' Chaim from Lomza, nor his rebbi's promise. He came to invite R' Chaim to his wedding.

"You told me ten years ago…" he reminded R' Chaim.

When R' Chaim heard the date that the wedding was scheduled for, he apologized to the *bachur*, saying that it would be impossible for him to attend on that day. "I beg your complete forgiveness," he said.

More than twenty years went by. That *bachur* was now a happy father about to marry off his son. Once again, he came to R' Chaim to invite him to the wedding.

Rav Chaim at a *chasunah*

R' Chaim replied, "Thirty years ago, I said that I'd come to your wedding and I didn't come. Therefore, even though you forgave me, I will, *b'ezras Hashem*, come to your son's wedding."

It was Purim, a time when people give one another *mishlo'ach manos* filled with wine and delicacies. The *bachurim* in Yeshivas Lomza, too, wanted to give *mishlo'ach manos* to their illustrious rebbi.

A Special Mishlo'ach Manos

For two years, they had been hearing a daily *shiur* from the *rosh yeshivah*, R' Elazar Menachem Mann Shach. Now they wished to give the *rosh yeshivah* a beautiful *mishlo'ach manos*.

"What should we give?" two *bachurim* asked each other. They were learning partners, *chavrusas*, and their names were R' Chaim Kanievsky and R' Dov Weintraub.

Finally, they devised a truly valuable *mishlo'ach manos*.

The two sat down and wrote comments on *Shas* — a comment on each tractate, in order, until *Bava Basra*. And they sent their commentary to R' Shach as their *mishlo'ach manos*.

Rav Chaim meets a bearded Purim guest

The *mashgiach* of Yeshivas Ponevezh, R' Avraham Grossbard, was sitting *shivah* following the *petirah* of his father, R' Shmuel Grossbard.

R' Chaim's Weapon

Hundreds of people came to the modest house to comfort the mourners for the death of their illustrious father.

One of the many people who came was R' Chaim Kanievsky. He had come to comfort the brokenhearted sons. This was a visit that had not been expected, and people wondered why he had decided to come.

R' Chaim solved the mystery the moment he sat down facing the surprised mourners.

"Do you know why I've come here today? Your father was my commanding officer in the army."

The surprise turned into astonishment. Their father in the army? And R' Chaim in the army? This was strange!

Quickly, he explained with a riveting story.

During Israel's War of Independence in 1948, yeshivah students received word from the newly formed government that a state of emergency had been declared. Everyone must go defend the borders of the brand-new State. No one was exempt.

The yeshivos heard the news in shock. What did they have to do with battlefields? But the order had left no room for questions. It must be obeyed.

The order came to Yeshivas Lomza as well, where many future *talmidei chachamim* were learning. The yeshivah's administrators appointed R' Shmuel Grossbard as captain of Lomza Company, which set out to mount a defense at the Egyptian border.

The Haganah (Israel's Army at the time) did not supply rifles or any other weapons. The only ammunition available were sticks and stones. The journey to the border was difficult. R' Moshe Soloveitchik cried copious tears all the way there. Everyone was afraid of the unknown that lay ahead. "When we reached the border," R' Chaim continued his tale, "R' Grossbard told me that I could go learn on the

A "Keren Hasheviis" gathering

hill. He just asked that I arm myself with a stick and some stones. And that's what I did.

"I took my Gemara and climbed to the top of the hill, where I learned until the skirmish was over.

"Today," he concluded, "I've come to say thank you to my commander for what he did for me. I am doing this through you, his sons."

And so, more than sixty years later, the story came to light: Torah during battle. Amazing.

Not at Any Price

People who see only with their eyes will happily accept any donation given to a Torah institution. Not so the *gedolei Yisrael*, whose view is crystal clear. They know when to accept *tzedakah* and when to push it away.

R' Chaim Kanievsky related that in the Chazon Ish's day there was a great need for money to cover the expenses of observing *shemittah* properly. Many people were poor. Enormous sums were needed to help the farmers who wanted to keep *shemittah* properly. Where would they find the funds to help them keep this important mitzvah?

It would be the first *shemittah* after the Israeli War of Independence in 1948, and in those early days, the mitzvah of *shemittah* was often ignored. People argued that it was impossible to observe it as it was written in the Torah. To defeat this outlook, it became even more urgent to find a regular source of funding to cover all the expenses of the coming *shemittah* year — 1951 — and bring peace of mind to those who wished to keep it properly.

The Chazon Ish sent R' Zelig Shapiro to handle this problem and raise the funds. Then a rich man who lived in Tel Aviv made a momentous announcement.

"I am prepared," he told R' Zelig, "to cover all the expenses of the *shemittah* year — on one condition. I want the Chazon Ish to come to a gathering in my home, even for only two minutes! I will give him the money at that gathering."

R' Zelig's legs carried him quickly to the Chazon Ish's home. Here was the money they needed, and it had come so easily! No more going around knocking on doors, no more explanations and requests for donations.

"A wealthy man who lives in Tel Aviv is prepared to donate the entire sum we need," R' Zelig related excitedly. "In return, he wants to make a gathering in the Chazon Ish's honor. He'd like the Chazon Ish to attend, even for only two minutes. Can I tell him that the Chazon Ish will come?"

To his astonishment, the Chazon Ish answered, "Absolutely not! I should go there just in order to receive money? That would dishonor the Torah. It is forbidden to do such a thing!"

The Chazon Ish didn't go. And the rich Jew did not donate a penny.

Fund-raising for *shemittah* continued with difficulty, but also with the knowledge that not everything that donors want must be

R' Elyashiv

done. Not if their demands contain even a kernel of dishonor to the Torah. At times you just have to say no.

When in the year 1951 a *shidduch* was suggested for R' Chaim Kanievsky with the daughter of the *posek hador*, R' Yosef Shalom Elyashiv, *zt"l*, the two men had never yet met.

What a Mechutan!

R' Chaim's father, the Steipler, had a friend named R' Shimon Yuzuk, *zt"l*, who had learned in yeshivah with the Steipler and now lived in Yerushalayim. The Steipler sent his friend a letter, asking if he was acquainted with the family of R' Elyashiv.

The answer was quick in coming: "If only *I* had such a *mechutan*!" That was enough for the Steipler.

Chapter 2: From the Lomza Yeshivah to Fatherhood / 33

R' Chaim, the young *chasan*

Many women came to Rebbetzin Batsheva Kanievsky, *a"h*, to ask for the secret of the double merit she enjoyed: being the daughter of the *posek hador*, R' Yosef Shalom Elyashiv, and — *yibadel l'chaim* — being the wife of R' Chaim Kanievsky, *shlita*, known to all as "Sar HaTorah," the Prince of Torah.

What's the Secret?

"What is the secret?" they asked. "Is the crown of Torah reserved only for *iluyim* — geniuses?"

"I don't know about geniuses," the *rebbetzin* answered, "but I can say one thing with clear knowledge. There is one thing that I have seen — breathed — all my life. And that is an unchanging reality — a reality that does not show the difference between day and night, between Shabbos and weekdays, between daily routine and days filled with troubles.

"The seconds, the minutes, the hours, the days, the weeks, the months, and the years — they are all parts of the pillar of *hasmadah*, of diligence in learning Torah, diligence and more diligence. That's how it was in my father's home, and that's how it was in the home I merited building after my marriage.

"Hashem gave me the *zechus* to build a home with a husband whose world contains nothing but the holy Torah. And it's that powerful *hasmadah* that has stood by him.

"There are no shortcuts on the way to the top of the mountain. Only a person who devotes all his time to climbing up that mountain will merit reaching its peak."

This, then, is the "secret": constant diligence, no matter what.

This advice, of course, is not easy to carry out, neither for the learner nor for his wife. And it does not happen overnight. Torah is acquired by putting together the seconds, the minutes, and fragments of hours of learning until they all add up to create a great light.

R' Chaim and Rebbetzin Batsheva Kanievsky's children grew up in a home where Torah was studied at every available minute in the day. Rebbetzin Batsheva used to say that even during their meetings before they were married, R' Chaim never stopped talking about Torah. He would speak to her about the *parashah.*

"*Baruch Hashem*, I was used to that. I grew up in a house where everything was Torah. I didn't know anything else. So I knew how to appreciate it and rejoice in the wonderful thing that had come my way."

After R' Chaim Kanievsky got married, he ran a cash *gemach* to help *kollel* men with their basic needs. One day, a poor *yungerman*

The Gemach came to him and asked for a loan of 750 lirot — a very large sum in those days.

R' Chaim gave him the full amount. A loan of that size cleaned out the *gemach.*

Just hours later, on that same day, along came a man who had deposited 750 lirot in the *gemach* as a loan. He had now come to take back his deposit. The *gemach* was empty, and R' Chaim didn't know what to do. The only way to raise such a large sum of money immediately was to go to the poor *yungerman* who had taken the loan and ask him to return it on the spot.

R' Chaim did not want to cause him such anguish. But he also couldn't ignore the man who had lent that money and wanted it back. It was his right to get back the money that he'd loaned the *gemach* on the day he needed it. What to do?

And then, for the third time that day, R' Chaim had dealings with that precise sum — 750 lirot. Totally unexpected, a man came and loaned the *gemach* that precise sum.

"Stories like these are lessons for us," R' Chaim said. "They teach us that in every matter, at every moment, Hashem is watching over us with precise *hashgachah pratis*!"

After his marriage, the administration of Yeshivas Tiferes Tzion, where R' Chaim had learned as a boy, asked him to give a *shiur* in the yeshivah.

"Not for You!"

He needed the money, and he thought that HaKadosh Baruch Hu had sent him a good opportunity. This way, he would have the merit of spreading Torah and also earn a respectable living. However, he would not make such a decision without asking for his father's consent.

R' Chaim consulted with his father, the Steipler. "That is not for you," his father told him firmly. "You sit and learn!"

The plan ended there.

From then on, over the course of all the blessed years of his life — may it be until 120! — R' Chaim continues to fulfill his father's advice: "You sit and learn!"

R' Eliyahu Mann, one of R' Chaim Kanievsky's *shamashim*, once said to R' Chaim, "They say that that someone once left a pen at the

Other People's Things

Steipler's house. After a year and a half, the same person came in. At once, the Steipler stood up and returned the pen to him. Did he really have such a great memory?" R' Mann asked.

"It came from a sense of responsibility," R' Chaim Kanievsky replied. He added, "After I was already married, I once went to my father's house and used a sheet of his paper without permission. Afterward, I brought paper from my house and put it down in place of the one I'd used.

Rav Chaim takes a walk

"Five years later (!), to my surprise, the sheet of paper that I'd brought was still lying where I'd left it. I asked my sister why they weren't using that paper. She said our father assumed that someone had forgotten the paper and left it there."

Two noble figures walked down the street near the Bnei Brak cemetery. They were the Chazon Ish and his nephew, R' Chaim Kanievsky.

Holy Ground Suddenly, the Chazon Ish spoke up. "In the spot where we are walking now, *talmidei chachamim* walked and spoke in learning. It has a special *kedushah*, a holiness that can be felt here."

Whenever R' Chaim repeated those words, he would add, "Such a level, in which a person can sense the *kedushah* of a place where Torah was learned, can only be achieved by learning the holy Torah itself."

R' Chaim Kanievsky was very close to the Chazon Ish for many years, and he followed his practices and opinions in every

In the Shadow of the Chazon Ish

situation. Every word that the Chazon Ish said or wrote was Torah and required study. R' Chaim remembered all of the Chazon Ish's halachic responses to those who came to him with questions.

A *yeshivah bachur* once went to see the Chazon Ish before Shavuos with a question. "Can I learn Gemara on Shavuos night, or do I have to say the *Tikkun*?"

He was referring to the *Tikkun Leil Shavuos*, a small *sefer* that has sections from the *Tanach* and Mishnah, certain texts from kabbalistic works, and a list of the 613 mitzvos.

"You can learn Gemara," the Chazon Ish replied.

Then another *bachur* asked the same question. But what was this? To this young man, the Chazon Ish said, "You can say the *Tikkun*. You don't have to learn Gemara."

This seemed very strange.

R' Chaim, who had witnessed both exchanges, remained puzzled until he thought about their questions. He realized that the different answers were linked to the way the questions were asked.

Rav Chaim reciting *Tehillim*

The first *bachur* wanted to learn Gemara, which was what he always did each Shavuos night. But he was afraid that it was more proper to say the *Tikkun Leil Shavuos*. To him, the Chazon Ish replied that he could learn Gemara.

The second *bachur*, on the other hand, wanted to say the *Tikkun*, which had been his custom up to that point, but thought that perhaps he should learn Gemara. The Chazon Ish told him that he could continue his custom and say the *Tikkun*.

Not only were the answers different, but so were the questions…

Bnei Torah often merit a special personal *hashgachah* in their lives. When the Chazon Ish was involved, this was often clear for everyone to see.

The Operation That Wasn't

One day, a young *yeshivah* *bachur* came to see the Chazon Ish. "The doctors say that I have to have an operation," the *bachur* said. "I've come to ask if I should listen to them, and to find out who I should ask to do the surgery."

The Chazon Ish asked the young man for some medical details, and then advised him to go ahead and have the operation. He also provided the name of the doctor he should see.

The *bachur* did not rise from his chair. If he had the privilege of being in the home of the holy Chazon Ish, why not seize the opportunity to talk to him about matters of Torah?

Immediately, the *bachur* began to relate his own *chiddushim* in

The Chazon Ish

Torah to the Chazon Ish. When he was done, the Chazon Ish declared, "You do not need an operation!"

The young man was stunned. "But the Rav just told me to have the surgery, and even told me who should perform it!"

"That is true," the Chazon Ish said. "But now I have seen that you are a *talmid chacham,* and Hashem runs things differently for a *talmid chacham.* You do not need an operation!"

The *bachur* accepted the new ruling just as he had accepted the first one. He did not have the surgery. *Baruch Hashem,* his condition was resolved without medical intervention.

Many years have passed since then, but everyone who was present in the room that day — including R' Chaim — remembers that incident as a foundation stone and vital lesson in the lives of *bnei Torah.*

From the time he was young, R' Chaim Kanievsky had the custom of observing *Yom Tov Sheini.* Most people in Eretz Yisrael observed **Taking Precedence** one day of *Yom Tov* on Pesach, Shavuos, and Succos. But R' Chaim also observed, on some level, the second day that was observed outside Eretz Yisrael. On those days, without noise or fanfare, he would not do any *melachah d'Oraisa* — work prohibited explicitly in the Torah.

One year, he departed from his usual custom and turned on a light on *Yom Tov Sheini.* What happened that year? Why had R' Chaim departed from his custom?

He did not turn on the light for his own need. He was in the home of his uncle, the Chazon Ish, who had asked him to turn on the light. On the spot, R' Chaim decided to do as the Chazon Ish had asked. After all, this fell under the category of giving honor to the *gadol hador,* and that is a *mitzvah d'Oraisa* — a mitzvah spelled out in the Torah.

Observing *Yom Tov Sheini,* on the other hand, is a *mitzvah d'Rabbanan* — from a rabbinical source. And for him, it was merely a stringency. And so, turning on a light, in this instance, took precedence over observing *Yom Tov Sheini.*

When R' Chaim Kanievsky was a young man, he toiled day and night to write down his *chiddushim* in Torah. Finally, the work was

Nachal Eisan

done. He'd succeeded in compiling his original Torah thoughts together and publishing them in a *sefer* called *Nachal Eisan*.

He took the *sefer* and brought it to his uncle, the Chazon Ish. Although the Chazon Ish did not read through the entire manuscript, he did study a few portions and wrote his comments on them.

Nachal Eisan had taken R' Chaim many years to write. In all, there were three editions of the *sefer*. The first two were shorter versions, while the third, written at length, was the one that was eventually published.

One day, a certain *talmid chacham* came to R' Chaim and said, "I learned your *sefer*, *Nachal Eisan*. Though the *sefer* is about the laws of *eglah arufah*, it has all sorts of other topics mixed in."

R' Chaim answered simply, "All of Torah is a single entity."

His words were modest. Because all of Torah is one entity, he implied, every Torah discussion touches on the entire Torah. R' Chaim was saying that his *sefer* is not special because it has so many topics, but it is a quality of the Torah that all topics are related.

It was a Friday night in the Kanievsky home, in the year 5714 (1953). Everyone was sound asleep in their beds. Suddenly, the noises

In the Middle of the Night

of morning were heard. Water pouring out for *netilas yadayim*, footsteps, rustling…

What was going on? Who had woken up? A brief investigation revealed that R' Chaim, a young man at the time, was ready to leave the house.

"What's the matter?" his *rebbetzin* asked. "Where are you going?"

"I'm going to daven *Shacharis*," R' Chaim said.

"Now? But it's still the middle of the night!"

"Really? It's the middle of the night?" R' Chaim asked in surprise. "I was sure that it was morning. I woke up and couldn't fall back

Rav Chaim and the Pesach matzos

asleep, so I assumed that it was almost dawn."

On *motza'ei Shabbos*, it was discovered why the Prince of Torah had suddenly woken up and been unable to fall back asleep.

At the very moment that he woke up that night, his uncle, the Chazon Ish, had passed from this world.

It was *erev Pesach* when a knock was heard at the home of R' Reuven Katz, *zt"l*, the *rav* of Petach Tikvah. He hurried to the door.

High-Quality Matzos

He knew who had arrived. In fact, he waited for him eagerly every year.

In the doorway stood the future Prince of Torah, R' Chaim Kanievsky, holding some matzos.

Each year, on *erev Pesach*, R' Chaim was sent to R' Reuven Katz's house to bring him special matzos baked by a *chaburah*, or group of men, in the Chazon Ish's oven.

Then came *erev Pesach* in the year 1954. That year, the matzos were baked by the same *chaburah* but, sadly, without the Chazon Ish, who had left this world just a few months earlier.

That year, too, R' Chaim Kanievsky came to R' Katz's house bearing matzos from the *chaburah*. R' Katz took them from him and asked, "This year, are the matzos as high quality as when the Chazon Ish was alive?"

R' Chaim answered, "Now they are of even superior quality. When the Chazon Ish was present, he would resolve our uncertainties by being lenient. Now that he is gone — we are stringent at every small doubt..."

The year was 1958. It was the first *shemittah* year since the *petirah* of the Chazon Ish.

The First *Shemittah* Storehouse

He had been the one who reestablished the mitzvah of *shemittah* in Eretz Yisrael seven years earlier. Under his direction, the Chazon Ish encouraged a group of farmers to observe *shemittah* and not to work their land. The Chazon Ish had dressed the mitzvah in the clothing of practical halachah. He had shown that one could observe the mitzvah of *shemittah* fully even today.

Now, after his passing, it was up to the public to safeguard this mitzvah and continue to keep it.

In the orchards, fruit was beginning to grow — holy *shemittah* fruit. Fruit that is grown during *shemittah* can't be sold to the public in the ordinary way. Because it has a special holiness, many other halachos apply to it as well. One *talmid chacham* went to his local *beis din* with a request to separate the fruit of the *shemittah* year. He wanted to make sure that the holy fruit of *shemittah* would be treated properly according to the halachah.

In order to do this for such vast quantities of fruit, the *beis din* had to get permission from Israel's Agricultural Ministry. But when the *beis din* asked the Agriculture Minister for the necessary permit, he turned them down. The ministry did not want to authorize a new process in selling fruit.

It was only after much effort and lobbying that the minister finally agreed to present the request to a special committee.

"You should know," one of the lobbyists for *shemittah* observance told the committee, describing a certain farmer, "that this man keeps his orchard going for six years, only in order to be able to make it *hefker* on the seventh!"

With these few words, he tried to provide the government with an alternate view: one in which a fruit's entire existence is for the merit of the mitzvos that involve it.

After a long and exhausting discussion, the committee finally agreed to establish an "Otzar Beis Din" to separate the *shemittah* fruits from the ordinary ones. Many issues had to be answered in order to make sure that the Otzar Beis Din could operate.

Where would the fruits be stored? Who was willing to provide space for them? Who was willing to undertake all the work and bother involved in the project? Who would agree to turn his home into a storage facility for so much fruit?

When Rebbetzin Kanievsky heard that a place was being sought for dividing the fruit of the Otzar Beis Din — along with a person to oversee the entire project — she didn't think twice. "I'll do it in my house!"

Before long, her small apartment, already crowded with young children, turned into the Otzar Beis Din's first storehouse in Eretz Yisrael.

She labored tirelessly. This volunteer job demanded long hours of hard work. "Let's pay her for her work," someone suggested.

But the *rebbetzin* firmly refused. "I am not prepared to receive a salary for this mitzvah here in this world," she said. "A treasure has fallen into my lap. I will not exchange it for coins of money!"

The Ponevezher Rav had a custom of closing registration to the yeshivah after a certain date. At that point, the yeshivah's gates were closed, and not another *bachur* could join for that year.

The Torah Itself

One day, a wealthy man who gave large sums of money to the yeshivah asked the Ponevezher Rav to accept his grandson into the yeshivah. This was after registration had already closed.

The Ponevezher Rav refused to accept the grandson, explaining to the rich man that registration was closed. He added that this applied to everyone; he did not show favor to one person over another.

Seeing that the *rav* refused to reconsider, the wealthy donor said, "If it's true that the times for registration are so strictly enforced, I have no complaints. However, if I should find out that there are exceptions, and other *bachurim* were able to get into the yeshivah, then I will not give another penny to Ponevezh Yeshivah!"

Just to make himself absolutely clear, he added, "The *rosh yeshivah* should know this: if I hear that a *bachur* was allowed to register late, I will not want to hear from the yeshivah again."

The Ponevezher Rav

Right after this conversation, the Ponevezher Rav walked out of the yeshivah together with R' Dovid Povarsky, one of the *roshei yeshivah*. As they walked down the stairs, they met the young R' Chaim Kanievsky climbing the stairs.

R' Chaim, seeing the *rosh yeshivah*, came up to him and said, "I've come to ask the *rosh yeshivah* to accept a relative of mine to the yeshivah…"

Without losing a beat, the Ponevezher Rav said, "I accept him."

They each went their separate ways. R' Povarsky, who had been a witness to both conversations, was astonished.

Just a few minutes before, the *rosh yeshivah* had refused a similar request from a man who donated enormous sums to the yeshivah. "Why," he asked the *rosh yeshivah*, "did you agree to accept R' Chaim's relative?" "R' Chaim is the Torah itself," the Ponevezher Rav replied. "I cannot refuse him…"

Even then, when R' Chaim Kanievsky was still a young man, he had earned the esteem and admiration of the Ponevezher Rav.

In This I Trust

It was a tense time. Israel's security situation was extremely precarious. From time to time there came the sound of shelling and the thunder of other weaponry.

The men sat in the Chazon Ish Kollel and learned. It was already past midnight when suddenly they heard the echo of mortar shells. The bombardment had begun!

The men in the *beis midrash* were frightened. They looked around, many thoughts racing through their heads. How would they step out into the street and go home when their learning was done for the night? What was happening at home right now?

Then they saw R' Chaim Kanievsky sitting in his place, bent over his Gemara as though nothing had happened. The others hurried over to him. How was it possible to continue peacefully learning, as though everything was just fine?

Torah. Only Torah.

R' Chaim answered them calmly. "The situation affects us only in one way. And that is the question of whether or not a tank can absorb *tumah*, impurity…"

So saying, he bent over the *sugya* again in utter and complete serenity.

"We saw with our own eyes," R' Reuven Fine, who had been there, exclaimed, "the fulfillment of the *pasuk* (*Tehillim* 27:3), *Im takum alai milchamah b'zos ani botei'ach* — 'If war should come upon me, in this I trust!'"

Chapter 2: From the Lomza Yeshivah to Fatherhood / 47

This story takes us back many years, to the time when R' Chaim Kanievsky was still a young man learning half the day in the Kollel Chazon Ish.

A Generous Stipend

He spent the *seder* writing his *sefarim*. But his hours of in-depth learning, research, and writing were regularly interrupted. He was constantly approached with questions in halachah or *hashkafah* or *mussar*. People wanted his advice, and they wanted his *berachos*.

But what about his learning? And what about his *sefarim*?

One day, a suggestion came. It was R' Avraham Genichovsky, who would become the *rosh yeshivah* of Yeshivas Kochav MiYaakov, who came to deliver it:

"A rich man came to me and asked that his name be kept anonymous," R' Avraham began. "It troubles this man that R' Chaim is constantly disturbed in his learning in the *kollel*. He has proposed to pay R' Chaim $1,000 a month. This is several times greater than the sum of money the *yungeleit* generally receive each month.

"This way, R' Chaim can learn at home and write his *sefarim* in peace, without all the constant interruptions."

The Prince of Torah

"I am very grateful for this person's goodwill," R' Chaim replied, "and I very much appreciate his offer. However, I do not want such an arrangement. When I learn in the *kollel*, while it's true that there are many interruptions as I'm writing, there is also some benefit. Each interruption forces me to go back to the start of the section and look at it afresh. So it turns out that the interruptions sharpen my work.

"Please give your generous, anonymous donor my thanks and tell him that I very much appreciate his good intentions."

Surrounded by Hashem's beautiful creations

R' Avraham Genichovsky got up to leave. R' Chaim, who wished to express his gratitude in more than just words, stood up to accompany him some distance, as a sign of his appreciation for the other man's concern.

R' Avraham left the house, and together the two men went out to the street. A few minutes later, a car stopped and the driver offered to give R' Avraham a ride home.

"Why did you decide to stop for me?" R' Avraham asked the driver humbly as he got into the car.

The driver answered, "Anyone whom the Prince of Torah accompanies out of the house — even for just a few steps — that's enough for me to know it's someone I should be picking up…"

What was going on here — a guided tour? Who was offering explanations as he moved from cage to cage?

A Unique Outing

It happened decades ago. One Chol HaMo'ed Succos, R' Chaim Kanievsky took his young children to the zoo. It was a special outing. In front of each cage, the father paused. While the people passing them by chatted idly,

R' Chaim explained to his children where the animal in each cage is mentioned in *Tanach* or in *Shas*.

From cage to cage, the audience of listeners grew larger. They understood that something like this doesn't happen every day. The crowd followed him around and along with his children they, too, drank in his words.

For all of them, this was a dual trip. It was a visit to the zoo and — over and above that — a trip down the byways of the Torah.

It was report-card time. Mrs. A. Friedland, the third-grade teacher, sighed.

Report Card Dilemma

Apart from all the work involved in actually filling out the report cards, it was also hard to decide what grades to give her students. While there were some girls who clearly deserved one mark or another, others required a great deal of thought. A girl could be very studious, but her grades were low because she wasn't adept at taking tests. Another always scored 90's on tests, but she talked during class.

The decision could go either way: she could act according to *middas hadin* — with strict justice — or with *middas harachamim*, with compassion. Which option to choose? And was one of the two choices the correct way to go in every case where the grade was in doubt?

She labored on the report cards for a while, trying to make the decisions on her own.

And then...it was time to fill out the report card of a student from a very illustrious family. That year, she had the privilege of teaching the daughter of R' Chaim Kanievsky, *shlita*.

Why should I hesitate? she thought. *I'll share my doubts with the girl's special mother and let her advise me.*

So the teacher took a sheet of paper and wrote a note to Rebbetzin Kanievsky.

"*Your daughter excels in all her studies,*" she wrote. "*However, she is quiet in class and does not participate enough. Should I grade her on her report card according to her knowledge, or take into consideration the fact that she does not participate much?"*

The girl brought the note home to her mother, and the teacher waited for an answer. What mark should she give the girl?

Even before the *rebbetzin* had a chance to answer, R' Chaim saw the teacher's note. On the spot, he wrote an answer:

"Please give my daughter the grades that she deserves. Do not show her any special favor."

The next day, the teacher read the words on the note, written by her student's illustrious father. She read it once, and then a second time. Each time, she was more moved. She was accustomed to receiving a very different kind of note from parents: notes that asked her to protect their child, to cushion them, to wrap their school life in cotton padding. And now — what a letter!

I will save this note in my purse, she decided. *It is a note that has emes — truth — speaking from between its lines.*

Not long ago, that teacher, the wife of R' Yosef Friedland, *zt"l*, passed from this world. Her family says that she saved that note till the last day of her life.

R' Chaim Kanievsky's home was steeped in Torah and halachah. That great household was built on Torah study and scrupulous mitzvah observance. It's no wonder, then, that even the young children — the girls as well as the boys — absorbed the importance of these values and tried to attain them in their own lives.

Two Halachos

"Abba," his young daughter once said. "I want to say two halachos every day."

After a moment, she added, "Short *halachos*."

Her father, R' Chaim, told her, "I have two short w for you. One, *Mishenichnas Adar marbim b'simchah* — 'When Adar comes, there is much rejoicing,' and two, *Mishenichnas Av mema'atim b'simchah* — 'When Av comes, we minimize rejoicing.'"

Measuring time in pages of Gemara

Rav Shach

Measuring Time

Every occupation has its own way of measuring time. A driver knows the distance he can cover in an hour. So does a sea captain and an airplane pilot. For them, an hour translates into a number of miles. The baker knows how many trays of bread he can bake in an hour. Time is translated into loaves of bread.

Talmidei chachamim have their craft as well. The Torah is their craft.

And the *talmid chacham*, too, measures time by how much he can accomplish.

One day, there was a problem with the water flow in the Kanievskys' building. The flow weakened to a trickle, and R' Chaim, who needed water, was forced to wait for the desired quantity to collect.

How does one calculate waiting time? By how much learning one can do!

In the time that it took for R' Chaim to collect the water he needed, he was able to learn the entire *Maseches Avadim*. On another occasion, when a similar problem occurred, R' Chaim said, "By the time there is enough water, a person can complete three pages of Gemara!"

R' Chaim at his father's *kever*

Even when R' Chaim Kanievsky was young, the *gedolei Yisrael* recognized his greatness in Torah and *yiras Shamayim.* They

The Prayers of a *Tzaddik*

realized that he had the power to be a *tzaddik* who decrees and has his prayers answered.

When Rav Yitzchak Zev Soloveitchik fell ill near the end of his life, he asked three *tzaddikim* to travel to the grave site of R' Shimon bar Yochai in Meron to daven for him.

Who were the three *tzaddikim* he asked to make the journey to Meron?

They were the Steipler Gaon, R' Shach, and — *l'havdil bein chaim l'chaim* — R' Chaim Kanievsky.

One day, the Steipler's daughter told her father, "Chaim's back is hurting him."

Kibbud Av Va'Eim — How Far?

The Steipler thought that she was talking about his son. R' Chaim was already married, so he went to R' Chaim's house and ordered him to get into bed. R' Chaim didn't understand the reason for this order, but because he was extremely careful with the mitzvah of honoring his father, he didn't even attempt to find out what was going on. Without a word, he got into bed.

"You have to rest," the Steipler told him. "Stay in bed until tomorrow morning."

When the Steipler returned home, he learned that his daughter had been referring to a different Chaim: R' Chaim Kluft, *shlita*, his granddaughter's husband.

Discovering the error, the Steipler said with a smile, "My son Chaim is liable to stay in bed until the morning ..." He knew how far his son's *kibbud av va'eim* extended.

The Steipler went back to R' Chaim Kanievsky's house and said, "You can get up!"

And just as he hadn't asked any questions about getting into bed, R' Chaim didn't ask any questions about getting out of it. He simply got up.

Now? Why not later? When I have the chance … Maybe tomorrow. Or perhaps next week. Sometime …

Why Not Now?

These are the arguments of the *yetzer hara*, as he tries to take our minds off our desire to do a mitzvah.

Our holy Sages dismissed the *yetzer hara*'s ploys with a single, decisive message: *Mitzvah haba'ah l'yadcha al tachmitzenah* — if a mitzvah is at hand, don't let it sit around!

When the *yetzer hara* starts raising questions and doubts, this message rises up immediately to wake us up. It tells us, "Here's your chance to do a mitzvah. Do it right now, without delay! If not, it may slip away and never return."

This was a message that R' Chaim Kanievsky has lived with all of his life. At all times and in any situation.

He does a mitzvah the minute it is possible to do it. He davens as soon as it is time to do so, makes the *berachah* on trees on Rosh Chodesh Nissan — the examples are endless.

One afternoon, R' Chaim returned home exhausted after a morning in the *kollel*. *But if a mitzvah is at hand, don't let it pass you by*! An answer had just come to him with regard to a question someone had asked him about a *shidduch*.

"I need to go and pass on the answer," he told his *rebbetzin* the minute he entered the house.

"Now? Maybe it would be better if you ate something and rested a little first..." the *rebbetzin* tried.

But R' Chaim turned around and left. "If I have the answer now, I won't put it off."

Don't let a mitzvah pass you by!

Up in Flames? An orange-blue flame merrily surrounded the top of the kerosene heater, spreading a pleasant warmth throughout the room. It was the height of winter, and the cold was penetrating. R' Chaim Kanievsky's daughter walked into the room to retrieve an article of clothing that had been drying near the heater. As she did so, a towel slipped and fell right onto the burning heater.

The *sefer*. Only the *sefer*.

In a flash, the flames shot up and set the towel on fire! Within short minutes, the fire had begun to spread.

Oh, no! What do I do now? the daughter wondered in alarm. Her mother, the *rebbetzin*, wasn't home. Only her father, R' Chaim, was there, learning in his room together with his friend and *chavrusa*, R' Berel Weintraub, *zt"l*.

Reluctantly, she knocked on her father's door — the only slight disturbance she would allow herself to make.

She knocked, but inside the room no one heard. In the meantime the flames were spreading, seizing hold of anything in its way.

The daughter knocked again and again. At long last, her father heard her and hurried to open the door.

"A fire!" the frightened girl said. "The kerosene heater set the room on fire!"

A woman who lived in the next building saw flames burst out of the window and reach the balcony. There was plenty of flammable material on the balcony. Many boxes sat there, filled with R' Chaim's new *sefarim*, ready for sale.

Oh no! the neighbor thought. *Soon the flames will reach the holy sefarim, which were written with such hard work and printed with hard work — and they'll devour them!*

But even before the fire trucks arrived, the neighbor witnessed a miracle.

The fire advanced until they were near the *sefarim*, and then the flames died down on their own. Not a single *sefer* was harmed!

Meanwhile, the *rebbetzin* returned home. We can imagine how stunned she was to see her home going up in flames. Downstairs, near their burning building, stood her husband, R' Chaim. His face was filled with joy.

"Why are you happy?" the *rebbetzin* asked him. A good question. Who feels happy in front of a burning house?

"This morning I finished writing a *sefer*," he explained. "I intended to bring the handwritten manuscript to R' Dov Landau later, so he

"Better than thousands in gold and silver..."

could review it. With special *hashgachah pratis*, I decided to send the manuscript to him immediately, the moment I finished writing it. I'm happy that the manuscript of that *sefer* is not in the house and will not be burned," R' Chaim joyously told his wife.

Nighttime. Someone knocked on the door and said, "I need to speak to R' Chaim."

Torah Amid Poverty

R' Chaim's wife, Rebbetzin Kanievsky, brought the man inside and led him to the doorway of a room. "You can go in," she said, motioning with her hand.

The man stood in the doorway as though rooted in place. He was having a hard time absorbing the sight he saw.

The room was completely covered by beds. The young Kanievsky children were asleep in them.

And in between all the beds sat R' Chaim learning Torah.

The man stood there, dumbstruck. He had never realized how poor the household was.

This was not a one-time event. The same scene repeated itself every night. It showed a family that was satisfied with little. The room seemed to announce, *Tov li Toras picha mei'alfei zahav vachesef* — "The Torah of Your mouth is better for me than thousands in gold and silver! (*Tehillim* 119:72)."

Among the many people who came at night to ask R' Chaim for his *psak* in halachah was one man who took out a camera and snapped a picture of that extraordinary scene. And then he published the picture in the newspaper.

A man named Mr. D. noticed the picture in the paper. It interested him very much. *Who knows?* he thought. *Maybe I will be Hashem's messenger to help the Kanievsky family! Perhaps I will be the one to have the privilege of bringing them relief.*

The newspaper had published the picture in order to teach the public the value of being satisfied with little, and had not been intended to serve as a fund-raising campaign. But the man longed to have a share in this awesome mitzvah.

HaKadosh Baruch Hu had blessed him with a great deal of money. It would be his privilege and pleasure to buy R' Chaim Kanievsky and his family a nice, big house.

With a heart filled with happiness, he went to the Kanievsky home.

"I'd like the great merit of buying your family a spacious house," the rich man said.

To his amazement, R' Chaim declined. "There's no need!" he declared.

The rich man did not want to let such a tremendous merit slip through his hands. So he tried a second time. When R' Chaim refused him again, he decided to try his luck with the *rebbetzin*. Women, he mused, have a better understanding of matters of comfort.

To his astonishment, he found the *rebbetzin* far from thrilled with his plan to improve their living conditions. "There's no need," she said firmly.

Still the rich man refused to give up. He went to R' Chaim's mother, the wife of the Steipler.

If R' Chaim's mother approved of his plan, perhaps it would finally be accepted by her illustrious son, if only out of respect for the mitzvah of *kibbud av va'eim*.

But here, too, the rich man didn't succeed.

"On the contrary," the *rebbetzin* told him, "it's good for people to come and see the difficult conditions under which R' Chaim and his family lives. Many poor Jews come to R' Chaim's home, and they learn that poverty and economic hardship do not have to impact a person's diligence and involvement in Torah. They come, and they learn that the Torah endures especially in those who limit their involvement in matters of this world.

"The sight resolves many of their doubts and eases their own ordeals. It answers such questions as 'We are lacking a livelihood. Maybe it would be worth my while to learn in a *kollel* that pays better, even if it would add less to my growth in Torah.' Or, 'Is it a good idea for my wife to take on a second job that would force me to stay home more than I've been doing until now?'

"All of these questions melt away at the sight of R' Chaim in his home."

Seeing that even R' Chaim's mother agreed with her son, he was forced to abandon his generous project.

In later years, someone found that photograph and asked Rebbetzin Kanievsky in surprise, "Was it really like this? This is how R' Chaim learned — surrounded by beds in which his small children were sleeping?" The *rebbetzin* replied, "Yes, that's exactly the way it was. But the camera didn't catch everything."

During that same period, the *rebbetzin* related, R' Chaim learned before dawn with his *chavrusa*, R' Yisrael Meir Erlanger, *shlita*. R' Chaim wanted his learning partner to sleep in his apartment so that he, R' Chaim, could wake him up before dawn each day and they could start learning right away. Despite the already overcrowded conditions, a bed was found for his *chavrusa* to use on a regular basis.

"And the idea of moving to a larger house?" the questioner continued.

"Yes, there was such an idea. Not just once, but a number of times during our life, people came to offer us a larger place to live. But we didn't accept their offers. It was better for us this way. *Baruch Hashem*, we didn't lack for anything," the *rebbetzin* concluded simply.

CHAPTER 3
The House on Rashbam Street

Waiting in a line is a fact of life in R' Chaim Kanievsky's house. Many people come to see him each day, and they all have to wait their turn to speak with him. For R' Chaim's helpers, the question keeps coming up: Who gets to go in first?

Honor the Scholars One day, two men came to see R' Chaim at the same time. One of them was a major monetary supporter of Torah who regularly supported five hundred kollel students. The other was a *talmid chacham* who learned in *kollel*.

The devoted grandson who lived in R' Chaim's house realized that each of these two visitors had a special value. He was at a loss. Which one came first? What to do?

But why decide for myself? he thought. *After all, I'm in the very best place to get the best answer to any question.*

At once, he went to his grandfather to report on who was waiting outside. He asked R' Chaim which one to admit first.

Without any hesitation, R' Chaim answered, "It's obvious that the *talmid chacham* takes precedence!"

Anyone who comes to see R' Chaim will see an unvarying sight: the Prince of Torah poring over a *sefer* and learning. Not only is the sight unvarying, so is the unending flow of advice that he gives to those who come to see him.

The Best Advice People come to R' Chaim with all sorts of problems: a sick relative, a difficult child, a desire for some encouragement and *chizuk*. Each one receives the personal advice that he needs. But along with that is a single suggestion that applies to every kind of life and every sort of problem. And that is *limud Torah* — the study of Torah.

Rebbes of eighth-grade boys ask, "How can we strengthen our boys, who just finished the eighth grade and have already been accepted into a yeshivah? It's natural for them to want to relax at this point, now that the hard work and stress of preparing for their entrance tests is behind them."

"Tell them," R' Chaim tells those teachers, "that those who learn now, after they've been accepted into yeshivah, will have success in yeshivah. But if they don't learn now, after they've been accepted, they will not succeed in yeshivah either. Because in order to succeed in the 'business' of Torah, one must learn constantly, and not only until they manage to achieve a certain goal."

Everyone comes to R' Chaim!

"I was born on the Steipler's *yahrtzeit*," a young boy told R' Chaim. "What am I obligated to do?"

The answer came promptly, "You should sit and learn well!"

Learn! Learn! This is the advice he gives the man who's afraid that he won't receive all the reward he expects to get in the next world. "When I learn *mishnayos* for the elevation of someone's soul, does that take away from my own reward?"

"The Chazon Ish was asked this question," R' Chaim says. "I will answer the way he did: 'What difference does it make to you? You are carrying out Hashem's will!'"

But when someone asks R' Chaim for his blessing for *yiras Shamayim*, fear of Heaven, he answers, "That is something I cannot do. *Yiras Shamayim* is something for which a person has to work on his own."

A Different Kind of Welcome

He was coming tomorrow. Tomorrow!

The next day would be a fateful one. The heads of the institutions had been awaiting this day for a long time and, even more, the reward it would bring with it.

Tomorrow, a very wealthy man was due to arrive In Eretz Yisrael. They very much hoped he would see fit to give their institutions a very nice donation.

How, they wondered, could they make his visit as pleasant as possible?

They gave a lot of thought to the question of how to welcome the rich man. It would certainly be a great honor for him to visit the home of the *gadol hador*, R' Chaim Kanievsky, *shlita*, and receive a *berachah* from him.

They spoke to R' Chaim's assistants. They explained the importance of this visit to a number of Torah institutions, and how they hoped for a donation from their guest.

The man arrived, and they welcomed him warmly. Then, as planned, he and the heads of the Torah institutions went to R' Chaim's home. R' Chaim's grandson passed on their request that R' Chaim receive the rich man.

The door opened, and the whole group entered. Confidentially, the heads of the institutions hoped that R' Chaim might say some words of praise about their institutions that would encourage the wealthy visitor to give generously to them.

But what was this? Were they hearing right? Oh, no!

They had worked so hard to soften the fellow up. What were their ears hearing now?

"The mitzvah of learning Torah is the most important one there is," R' Chaim told the rich man. "Do you have time to learn?"

The wealthy visitor was no less surprised than the men who had accompanied him. He had been all ready to hear plenty of compliments about his great work on behalf of Torah institutions. But this?

The man cleared his throat. "Me?" he mumbled. "I'm so busy ..."

R' Chaim saw fit to rebuke him. "It's not possible," he said, "for a Jew not to set aside time to learn Torah. *You* must find time to learn as well," he told his visitor.

The heads of the delegation shifted uncomfortably in their seats. What would happen now? Would the man be willing to donate anything after the rebuke he'd just been given? This was something they had not expected at all.

But their fears were groundless. Later, when the wealthy man's welcoming ceremony was behind them, he told the heads of the institutions that the most enjoyable part of all for him was the time he'd spent in the home of R' Chaim Kanievsky.

Through the open door came a stream of people to comfort the mourners. The S. family was a traditional one and now the father had

Nachas to the Departed

passed away.

The days of *shivah* are a time for introspection. Now and then, the comforters would urge the mourners, "You must be strong!" The teenage son took these words to heart. At the end of the *shivah*, he went to see R' Chaim Kanievsky for guidance.

"They told me that I must strengthen myself," he said. "But I don't know how. What must I do?"

"How do you spend your time?" R' Chaim asked.

"I spend most of the day at work, but I set aside time to learn *Chumash* each day. I also listen to *mussar* talks for half an hour."

"That's not enough," R' Chaim said. "You must learn Gemara regularly for an hour or two each day."

Gemara? The young man was alarmed. "How will I know how? I've never learned Gemara in my life!"

"If you want to give your father *nachas*, take a *chavrusa* to learn with you. Learning Gemara," R' Chaim told the bereaved young man, "is the way to give *nachas ruach* to the departed."

A Different Kind of Cure

The family doctor studied the patient. He felt here and there, and then pressed his lips together, puzzled. This was strange. He had never seen a case like this.

"I'm sorry," he told the 20-year-old young man standing before him. "I don't know why your face has become twisted. I can't help you. I'd like to send you to a specialist."

So saying, he began writing a referral to a different doctor.

The young man waited impatiently for his turn with the specialist. Everywhere he went, people stared at him and asked him curious questions:

"What happened to your face?"

"What does the doctor say?"

"What can be done?"

All in all, an unpleasant situation.

If only this specialist will be Heaven's messenger to help me, he hoped.

To his disappointment, the specialist was equally at a loss. With raised brows he said, "An unusual case. I have no idea what has

"A beard is the glory of the face"

caused your face to become so twisted. There's nothing I can do to help you."

The young man's parents continued to look for medical help, but the third and fourth doctors they consulted were as unsuccessful as the first two in finding the root of the problem.

Upset, the young man decided to go see the *gadol*, R' Chaim Kanievsky.

"My face has become twisted," he told R' Chaim, "and the doctors can do nothing!"

"Grow a beard, and your face will get back in order," R' Chaim said.

A beard? the youth thought in astonishment. *What does a beard have to do with healing my face?*

R' Chaim explained:

"The Gemara in *Maseches Shabbos* says that a beard is the glory of the face. You have denied yourself this glory by shaving off your beard so, *middah keneged middah*, the beauty of your face has been taken away. Resolve to grow a beard, and healing will come."

The young man did as R' Chaim advised. He grew a beard, and his face righted itself!

Time passed. One day, a bearded youth came to the Kanievsky house. "I'm the one whose face was all twisted," he announced with great joy. "*Baruch Hashem*, I did as the *rav* advised, and my face went back to normal! I've come now to announce that I've just become engaged."

Grinding the flour for matzahs

How do our human eyes view things? Apparently, very differently from the way our *gedolim* do.

Another Room — Another Half-Hour

One day, a man came into R' Chaim Kanievsky's house to ask his advice.

"I have to choose between two possibilities," the man said. He was talking about his search for an apartment for his family.

"One option is to buy an apartment in a central location, close to everything. But such a place will be very expensive. With the money I have available, I'd only be able to buy a small apartment.

"The second option is to buy an apartment in a far-off place that's less in demand. The prices are not as high there, and I'd be able to buy a bigger place."

Chapter 3: The House on Rashbam Street / 67

"Why do you need a large apartment?" R' Chaim asked him. "Why do you need another room for *bedikas chametz*? A larger apartment will add an extra half-hour each year to your search for *chametz*."

With these words, his visitor was transported to another world. A world in which an extra room was not a physical concept but a halachic one, related to the search for *chametz* before Pesach each year.

If the bed stands here, it will block the closet's left-hand door. And if the bed stands near the window, the child will be cold. Perhaps a bunk bed?

Just Like Heleni HaMalkah

Or maybe the time has come to look for a larger apartment? We're so crowded here!

The father of a family, a man who learned Torah all day long, decided to consult with R' Chaim Kanievsky.

"Our apartment is small," the *yungerman* told R' Chaim. "We have many children, *kein yirbu*. Maybe we should move to a different apartment?"

Plenty of room in a small space!

R' Chaim and
R' Elyashiv

R' Chaim replied, "Have you learned *Maseches Succah*? In *Maseches Succah*, it says that Heleni HaMalkah had seven children, and they all lived in very small rooms.

"They managed. And you can, too!"

The power of *berachos*

R' Lipa Yisraelson, *shlita*, sat quietly near the *posek hador*, R' Yosef Shalom Elyashiv, *zt"l*, waiting for him to speak.

Blessings He had come to consult with R' Elyashiv about a dangerously ill patient. At the end of the discussion, R' Elyashiv said, "In each generation, there is a power of *berachos* that descends to the world. In our generation, that power has been given to R' Chaim Kanievsky. Go to him now and ask him for a *berachah* for the patient."

R' Lipa Yisraelson went immediately to R' Chaim and told him about the sick man. He added R' Elyashiv's words about R' Chaim's blessings.

"And *I'm* telling you," R' Chaim said, "that the power of *berachos* was given to my teacher and father-in-law, R' Elyashiv!"

The *berachos* of *tzaddikim* that the patient merited that day sustained him for two more years of life.

A young *kallah* came down with a serious illness just a short time before her wedding. Urgently she was flown out of the country to undergo an operation.

"I Knew…" One of her relatives went to the Kanievsky home and wrote the girl's name on a slip of paper so that R' Chaim would daven for her speedy recovery.

A few days later, the surgery proved a failure and the girl passed away. That same relative sadly returned to tell R' Chaim.

R' Chaim said, "I knew it would end this way. The minute you told me of her illness, I was prepared to daven for her during *Shemoneh Esrei*. But each time, the matter would fly out of my head and I forgot. Even when I put the slip of paper with her name into my siddur, the paper got lost. So I knew that she had been decreed for death."

The deal was struck. The apartment's owner and its prospective buyer sat down to write a memo outlining details of the sale.

Sage Advice Before the contract was signed, the seller went to the Kanievsky home to tell him that he was selling his apartment and going to live in another city.

"Do not leave Bnei Brak!" R' Chaim advised.

The seller didn't know what to do. He had already reached a decision, found a buyer, and even written a memo saying that he intended to sell the apartment to him.

"It was in the merit of your *emunah* ..."

He decided to come to a compromise with the buyer that would allow him to cancel the sale. A short time later he discovered that, had he sold the apartment then, he would have lost a fortune! He had planned to sell the apartment in exchange for dollars, while the place he'd intended to buy was being sold in shekels. In that period of time, the value of the dollar unexpectedly fell sharply; had the sale gone through, he would have lost the astronomical sum of $40,000!

"The *rav* saved my money," the man told R' Chaim gratefully.

"It was not in my merit," R' Chaim responded. "It was in the merit of your *emunah* that you did not come to financial harm."

R' Chaim went on to relate the following story.

A woman in distress once came to the Chazon Ish's house. She stood at one side of the room and bitterly described all the suffering that weighed on her heart.

When those present saw the woman ranting on about all her problems and disturbing the Chazon Ish's learning, they wanted to send her out of the room. But the Chazon Ish stopped them.

"Let her be," he said. "See how much *emunah* there is here. This woman believes that, by airing all her problems in a place where Torah is being learned, she will find salvation for all her troubles."

See how much emunah there is here!

"Rebbe, I'm marking a *yahrtzeit* this week," someone told R' Chaim Kanievsky. "I'd like to daven for the *amud* on the *motza'ei Shabbos* preceding the *yahrtzeit*, but another member of the *minyan* is an *avel* (in mourning) this year. Who should take precedence — him or me?"

Elevation for the Soul

R' Chaim answered, "They say that R' Yisrael Salanter was once in the same kind of predicament, and he gave up his right to lead the davening. He was asked, 'How could you give it up? After all, davening for the *amud* brings about an elevation for the deceased person's *neshamah.*'

"R' Yisrael Salanter replied, 'To be *mevater*, to give something up for someone else, is also a mitzvah. It can also serve to elevate the *neshamah*!'"

The *rav* came to give his daily *shiur* in *daf yomi* and sat down in his place. Strange. What was going on today?

Which Daf?

Every day, the other men would be sitting and learning with open Gemaras by the time he walked in. Where was everyone today?

Maybe I came early, he thought. *Maybe my watch is fast.*

The *rav* sat and waited … and waited … but no one came. Dismayed, he closed his Gemara, put it back on its shelf, and went back home.

The next day, everything went smoothly. The men were waiting in their seats when the *rav* arrived. He came in, opened his Gemara, skipped a page, and began teaching.

The men did not want to lose out on the missing page. Though they had not shown up for the *shiur* the day before — each one for reasons of his own — now they wanted to learn yesterday's *daf*. But the *rav* continued on as before. It didn't matter to him if people came or didn't come. Yesterday's *daf* was yesterday's *daf*, and today's *daf* was today's *daf*!

After the *shiur*, one of the participants decided to ask R' Chaim Kanievsky what was the right thing to do. To learn yesterday's *daf*, or today's?

R' Chaim replied, "You are all correct.

"The students are correct because it's their right to fill in the material they missed.

"And the *rav* is right, too. By doing what he did, he was teaching the students that one does not miss a Torah *shiur* for anything. A *shiur* that they do not learn remains irreplaceable!"

R' Chaim's answer helped the men understand the reasoning behind the *rav*'s decision.

Looking back, that was a lesson all on its own.

They had just learned that *bitul Torah* is a loss that can't be made up.

"One does not miss a Torah *shiur* for anything"

On his way from shul

The *talmid chacham* sat in front of his Gemara, his *shtender* pulled toward him and his thumb pointing up. "Aha ... aha ..." he murmured with satisfaction as he delved into an interesting question.

An Urgent Question

He tried to get to the bottom of the issue. *I'll go over to R' Chaim Kanievsky's house and present him with my question*, he thought. *Very interesting. I'm curious to hear what he'll say.*

He got up and went out to the street, his lips still murmuring the fine points of the question. In a few minutes he would spread his thoughts on the table in front of R' Chaim.

When his turn came, he laid out his question and then presented his answer. As he spoke, he looked at R' Chaim's eyes, hoping to see a sign that R' Chaim approved of what he was saying. To his disappointment, the look he wanted to see wasn't there. The issue he had presented was about a case that could never happen.

"What difference does this question make?" R' Chaim asked.

"Well ... it's about understanding the *pshat*, the simple meaning, of the *Minchas Chinuch*," the man answered.

Instead of discussing the issue itself, R' Chaim told him a story.

"One day in shul, in the middle of *chazaras hashatz*, a man came to stand next to me. It was obvious that he had some urgent matter that couldn't wait.

"'I have an urgent question,' the man said.

"As we all know, there are urgent questions of *pikuach nefesh* — life and death. For such questions, we can certainly interrupt our davening. 'What's the question?' I asked.

"'What is the halachah,' he asked, 'if a person is born with two heads? On which of them does he wear his *tefillin*?'"

What an "urgent question" to ask in the middle of *chazaras hashatz*!

"I told him," R' Chaim concluded, "that he should put *tefillin* on both heads for now, and we'll talk again later."

With this story, R' Chaim was explaining to the man who'd come to see him that in learning, too, we must stick with what is possible and probable. The search for truth must march hand in hand with reality.

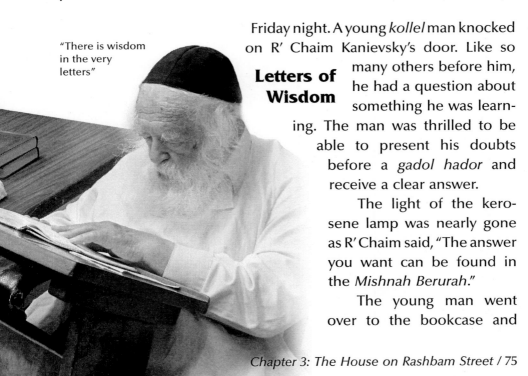

"There is wisdom in the very letters"

Letters of Wisdom

Friday night. A young *kollel* man knocked on R' Chaim Kanievsky's door. Like so many others before him, he had a question about something he was learning. The man was thrilled to be able to present his doubts before a *gadol hador* and receive a clear answer.

The light of the kerosene lamp was nearly gone as R' Chaim said, "The answer you want can be found in the *Mishnah Berurah*."

The young man went over to the bookcase and

brought the *sefer* to R' Chaim. But it was too dark for R' Chaim to read it.

"It's hard for me to strain my eyes to read these small letters," he told his visitor. "Come back tomorrow, and I'll read what the *Mishnah Berurah* has to say."

But the man wanted to leave with an answer tonight. So he suggested that he read the words of the *Mishnah Berurah* to R' Chaim, and R' Chaim could then explain them.

But R' Chaim did not consent to this idea.

Placing a hand on the young man's shoulder, he said pleasantly, "I want to read the words myself. There is wisdom in the very letters."

What is the peak of happiness for a *ben Torah*? What is the highest level that he can try to reach?

The Peak of Happiness

Anyone who lives a Torah life knows the right answer to this question: what can be more satisfying than sitting and learning Torah? Still, there are moments in life when a burning desire fills a man's heart — to have the merit of teaching Torah, to be a *rosh yeshivah*.

From time to time, a *ben Torah* will come knocking at R' Chaim Kanievsky's door and pour out his heart about how sad he is that

"To sit and learn is the best thing"

he does not have the merit of spreading Torah. To each of them, R' Chaim confides, "Do you know how many times in my life I've been offered the post of *rosh yeshivah*? Naturally, each time I went to my father, the Steipler, to ask his advice. His opinion was always the same: 'You need to sit and learn!'"

With a look of pleasure on his face, R' Chaim adds, "It's a miracle that my father did not approve. This way, I could continue sitting and learning."

Then R' Chaim tells his visitor, "I advise you to do the same thing. Sit and learn, and all will be well."

"Me?" the *kollel* man asks bitterly. "Does anyone even want me to be a *rosh yeshivah*?"

"Be glad they don't want you," R' Chaim says. "To sit and learn is the best thing!"

The Main Thing

A *bachur* once asked R' Chaim, "I learn a certain number of pages of Gemara every day. Which *masechta* is it best for me to learn within this framework: a short one that will let me start and finish an entire tractate, or a different *masechta* that's not especially short, and which I won't get to finish?"

"It makes no difference," R' Chaim told him. "The main thing is to learn!"

Passing the Test

A *yeshivah bachur* came to R' Chaim Kanievsky's home seeking advice.

"I have to travel out of the country," he explained. "I know that the trip will be filled with spiritual dangers. What should I do in order to be saved from the tests that will bombard me every place I go?"

"I can give you three suggestions," R' Chaim replied. "First, you must be involved in learning Torah. Second, you must learn *mussar*. And my third piece of advice: come back to Eretz Yisrael!"

Torah protects us, and *mussar* protects us, but a person's *yetzer hara* can still overpower him. This is where the third piece of advice

In letters or in person, everyone comes to R' Chaim for advice

R' Chaim wearing his *tefillin*

comes in: we have to make sure to put ourselves in the type of environment that helps us pass our tests!

Right and Left

The doctor's grim expression did not bode well. The mother had asked the usual question that one asks after giving birth: "Is my baby all right?" In the past, with her other children, a reassuring answer had been quick to come.

But not this time.

"The baby had a problem with her breathing," the doctor said. "They gave her a little oxygen."

He didn't want to say anymore to the woman so soon after childbirth.

Instead, the doctor spoke to the baby's father.

"Look," the doctor told the new father, "your baby has a heart defect. The left and right chambers have switched places. She will need a complicated operation to rearrange the structure of her heart."

Stunned by the news, the father decided to ask his relatives to go to R' Chaim Kanievsky and ask his advice. What could be done to ensure the success of the operation and his newborn daughter's speedy recovery?

R' Chaim thought about the question for several moments. Then he said, "Let the new father buy a pair of *tefillin* for an orphan or a new *ba'al teshuvah*."

He explained:

"You would think that the Torah would have told a person to wear *tefillin* on his right arm, which is the dominant one. But despite the importance of the right hand, HaKadosh Baruch Hu switched things around and gave supremacy to the left arm instead. By buying *tefillin* for another Jew, the father will merit having Hashem switch his daughter's right and left [chambers of the heart] as well."

Upon hearing this advice, the father went to see a Jew he knew, a man who had recently been showing signs of wanting to draw closer to *Yiddishkeit*.

"Do you know a *ba'al teshuvah* who might be interested in starting to put on *tefillin*?" he asked.

"Uh …" the man stammered. "Um … I … actually … I wasn't thinking about putting on *tefillin* … But now that you ask, I am ready to undertake to put on *tefillin* for the rest of my life so that your daughter will get well!"

The father wasted no time. He hurried off to buy the man an expensive pair of *tefillin*.

And when the time came, the surgery was completed with success.

The Right Answer?

Not every *yeshivah bachur* has the experience of floating on air. This *bachur* walked through the streets of Bnei Brak bursting with happiness. In just a little while, he would reach the home of R' Chaim Kanievsky. In a few minutes he would have the privilege of sharing with that Torah giant what he had achieved in his Torah learning.

The words flew from his mouth, and it seemed to him that a sweet, joyous melody accompanied them. "I've had the merit of learning a complete cycle of *daf yomi. Baruch Hashem*, I've finished. Now I'd like to ask what I should learn next. Should I learn the *daf yomi* of the *Talmud Yerushalmi* — or start a new cycle of *daf yomi* from the *Talmud Bavli*?"

"What is the last *masechta* you learned?" R' Chaim asked.

"*Maseches Niddah*," the *bachur* replied.

R' Chaim asked him a question from the *masechta*, and the *bachur* answered.

"Are you sure that's the right answer?"

The *bachur* hesitated. "N … no. I'm not sure."

"In that case," said R' Chaim, "go back and learn *Talmud Bavli* again."

When the *bachur* returned to his yeshivah, he immediately opened up a Gemara to *Maseches Niddah* and checked his answer. To his joy, he found that it had been correct.

He decided to go back and consult R' Chaim again.

"About the question from *Maseches Niddah*," he said to R' Chaim, "the answer I gave was the correct one."

"True," said R' Chaim. "The answer was correct, but you had no confidence in it. The words of Torah should instantly roll off your lips. It's best that you learn another cycle of *Talmud Bavli*!"

"How old is your oldest son?" R' Chaim asked the man who had come to see him.

Who Is a Good Father?

"He is 21," the father answered.

"What does he learn?" R' Chaim asked.

"I don't know."

"A father should know what his son is learning," R' Chaim admonished. "He should take an interest and test him now and then."

"He's big already," the father said to defend himself.

"A father has to
know what his
son is learning!"

But R' Chaim insisted. "It doesn't matter how old he is. A father
has to know what his son is learning!"

On that day, the man learned that a father may supply everything
his son needs, but as long as he doesn't take a personal interest in
his son's learning, despite all his worry and hard work, he is not yet
a good father!

Could it be true? So young, and he'd already completed the
entire *Shas*? Wow! People were impressed. What an accomplishment
for such a young *bachur*!

No Room for Ayin Hara

Then they started worrying: maybe it would
be better not to talk about it? Should they be
afraid of an *ayin hara*? This was the question that the boy's relatives
brought to R' Chaim Kanievsky.

But R' Chaim saw no problem. To finish *Shas* just once and be
afraid of an *ayin hara*? Can a person really "own" *Shas* — with an
eternal ownership — merely by learning it one time?

Intense concentration

R' Chaim Kanievsky's family witnesses his incredible concentration when learning Torah daily. While he is learning, it is as though

What Concentration!

he is in a different world. At such times, he hardly senses anything around him.

The same scene repeats itself over and over. People from his household will go to his room to ask him a question. But even after they enter and start talking to him, it takes time before he actually senses their presence.

One family member, whose responsibility it is to go back and forth bringing people and their questions to R' Chaim, describes a scene that has become routine by now: the question is asked, but R' Chaim continues learning as though he hasn't heard a thing. The questioner stands there, waiting silently for an answer. Waiting … and waiting …

Minutes pass, but nothing happens. During those minutes, the questioner gets to see a shining example of absorption in Torah, to a degree unparalleled in our time.

After a long wait, R' Chaim finally notices that someone is standing there. "Did you want something?" he asks.

And that is when the questioner realizes that the question he just asked out loud was not heard at all. Because every ounce of R' Chaim's attention was completely focused on the depths of the material he was learning.

Mail Call at Rashbam

As the mailman approaches a certain address, he knows that his mailbag will soon become considerably lighter. He has a huge stack of letters, all addressed to 23 Rashbam Street — home of the Prince of Torah, R' Chaim Kanievsky.

As soon as the mailman completes his job, another long and complicated task begins inside the house.

Letters to the Prince of Torah

The letters are sorted into piles, each of them awaiting an answer: questions in halachah, questions about how to act in a certain situation, questions on *hashkafah* and *mussar*, requests for advice, personal questions and community ones. Letters from nearby and letters from far away.

So many letters! How is it possible to answer them all?

"Answering letters from *bnei Torah*, either with words of encouragement or with answers to halachic questions, actually falls into the category of *chesed*," R' Chaim explained.

"My father, *zatzal*," he went on, "used to answer every letter to strengthen *bnei Torah*. And he would add, 'We don't know in what merit we are living. We must increase our merits!'"

And so, every day, R' Chaim has the merit of sending out his answers, which involve all areas of Torah, *Shas*, and the *poskim*.

One of his grandsons once asked him, "Why not continue writing your *sefer*, *Derech Chochmah*? Wouldn't that be a great merit for many people? Why spend so much time writing letters to individual people instead?"

R' Chaim replied, "Because the letters, too, have great public merit. My son, R' Shaul, *shlita*, publishes them in a *sefer* called *Da'as Nota*, so they reach many people."

When R' Chaim finished writing his *sefer* in the winter of 5767 (2007) and he was very busy preparing the manuscript for publication, even then he didn't completely abandon the holy work waiting for him in the many envelopes that came to his house each day. He continued answering them, despite the great burden of replying to ten letters a day.

Who were those ten lucky recipients?

The first people R' Chaim made a point of answering were Kohanim. A person with the name Cohen or Kahan fell into this category, on the assumption that the sender was a Kohen.

Most of the letters R' Chaim receives are from people he doesn't know. But when someone sends him a letter containing original Torah thoughts, he takes the person's words to his heart and feels as if the writer was someone he has known for years.

Once, picking up a Torah pamphlet, he saw an article by a *rav* who had since passed away. R' Chaim hadn't known him at all. Nevertheless, he said, "I remember him. He wrote Torah *chiddushim* in a book that was published in Yerushalayim."

About half a century had passed since he had been "introduced" to this unknown person, but because R' Chaim had once read that *rav's* Torah thoughts, the *rav* had become unforgettable.

Hundreds of letters lie on R' Chaim Kanievsky's desk, all of them awaiting an answer. But even writing a brief response takes a lot of work.

What's in a Title?

One day many letters came, all from the same place. A certain fine *kollel* man in Yerushalayim kept sending letter after letter, each one with its own question in learning.

R' Chaim could not handle so many questions from one source. In his humility, he apologized to the writer, saying that he did not have the ability to respond to so many questions in learning. In his letter of response, R' Chaim begged the other man's forgiveness, adding that he could see from the man's letters that he was a great *gaon* in Torah.

Everyone waits for R' Chaim's answer

A family member who saw this letter expressed his surprise. A great *gaon* in Torah? What, he wondered, had that *kollel* man done to deserve such a title?

"So what?" R' Chaim answered simply. "They write the same things to me …" In his great humbleness, he judged the use of such titles as not meaningful because people also referred to *him* this way!

On another occasion, R' Chaim received a letter from a young *bachur*. In the letter, the boy called R' Chaim "*Maran rabban shel kol bnei hagolah*" — the leader of all the Jews of the diaspora.

In his letter of response, R' Chaim addressed the boy the same way. "To *Maran rabban shel kol bnei hagolah*."

"But why?" someone asked him. "Why does that *bachur* merit such a title?"

"It's nothing," R' Chaim said. "He wrote that to me — so I wrote the same thing to him."

"I didn't know they put in an air conditioner"

Air Conditioners and *Berachos*

There was a new air conditioner in R' Chaim Kanievsky's house. It was a replacement for the old one, which was broken.

"Did the *rav* make the *berachah* of *hatov u'meitiv* on the new air conditioner?" someone asked him.

"I didn't know they switched air conditioners," R' Chaim replied.

"Well, when they put in the *old* air conditioner," the questioner pressed, "did the *rav* make the *berachah* then?"

"I didn't know they put in an air conditioner."

The questioner left R' Chaim's room without knowing whether or not

R' Chaim thought that one should recite the blessing of *hatov u'meitiv* over a new air conditioner.

But he *had* learned just how deeply one can be absorbed in Torah!

"I need advice and a *berachah*," the principal of a Talmud Torah in Eretz Yisrael told R' Chaim Kanievsky one day. "Our *cheder* has major financial problems. I'm thinking about traveling out of the country to raise funds for our school."

A Strange Blessing

"You can make the trip," R' Chaim replied. "And I give you a *berachah* that you will *not* succeed!"

The principal opened his eyes wide in astonishment. "What kind of *berachah* is that?"

"If you do not succeed," R' Chaim explained, "then you will not fly out of the country again. This is a big blessing. But the trouble you take now, and the efforts you make here in Eretz Yisrael, will bring salvation from another source!"

"My son will become a bar mitzvah soon," a father said. "I want to bring him to R' Chaim Kanievsky for a *berachah*."

A Strange Question

A few days later, father and son came excitedly to the Kanievsky home. Here was the day they'd been waiting for, when the boy would receive a *tzaddik's berachah* as he prepared to accept the yoke of mitzvos.

The father was very surprised when R' Chaim turned to him and asked, "And you? Have *you* had a bar mitzvah already?"

Why would R' Chaim ask such a question? Most people assume that a father of a bar mitzvah had his own bar mitzvah when he was a boy. It hung in the air, as the father tried — unsuccessfully — to figure out what had made R' Chaim ask him that question.

Even after he left R' Chaim's house, the question continued to trouble him. Why *had* R' Chaim asked him such a question? It made no sense! Could anyone think that he, the father of a bar mitzvah boy,

A bar mitzvah boy gets a *berachah*

had never celebrated his own bar mitzvah? The question remained a riddle.

Years passed. The man's grandmother was a *giyores*, a convert to Judaism. One day, a question arose regarding her conversion.

The question was brought to the great *posek*, R' Nissim Karelitz, *shlita*, who ruled that — just in case — the grandmother's descendants should undergo conversion, too.

Now that the father was required to undergo conversion, he remembered R' Chaim's long-ago question. He realized that the question had not been inexplicable or illogical at all; if there was a question of if he was a Jew or not, then perhaps he hadn't really had a bar mitzvah yet! The question that had been asked all those years before now made perfect sense.

A Strange Hunger

On the table were half a loaf of bread, a bowl of salad, and containers of yogurt, cheeses, and spreads. The boy washed his hands and sat down to eat.

"An egg?" offered his mother.

"Yes, thank you," the boy replied.

Slice followed slice. The salad bowl quickly emptied. The egg was received with thanks and gobbled up in an instant.

"I've noticed something interesting," the boy's mother told his father afterward. "Lately, our son is eating enormous amounts of food."

"I've noticed the same thing," the father said worriedly.

"Is there any more bread?" the boy asked at mealtime the next day. His mother was astonished to see that he had eaten all the bread that had been on the table and was still hungry!

He claimed to be hungry between meals as well. After a full meal, he would fill in the void with cookies and fruit.

"Could he be suffering from some kind of medical condition?" the anxious parents asked their doctor.

"Attacks of hunger can be a symptom of illness," the doctor acknowledged. He suggested that they run some tests.

A blood test showed that, *baruch Hashem*, the boy was healthy.

"It will pass," the doctor comforted them. "Sometimes, when going through adolescence, a boy needs greater quantities of food."

But the parents remained worried. They, too, had been adolescents once, and they knew that this hunger of their son's was something out of the ordinary.

The anxious father decided to consult with R' Chaim Kanievsky.

"Our son eats and eats without stop. He never feels full. We don't know — and neither does the doctor — what's behind this hunger!"

"Check the mezuzos," R' Chaim advised.

The father did as R' Chaim had suggested and brought their mezuzos in to be checked. To his shock, it turned out in that one of the mezuzos in their house, instead of saying the words *v'achalta v'savata*, "you shall eat and be satisfied," it mistakenly read, *v'achalta v'achalta*, "you shall eat and you shall eat!"

The barber had his hands full. The line was long, and the work was nonstop. Everyone seemed to be coming in today.

A Haircut in Honor of What?

This was nothing new for either the barber or his customers. It was the day before 17 Tammuz. Starting tomorrow, it would be forbidden to get a haircut for the next three weeks. So was it any wonder that everyone was coming in for a haircut today?

R' Chaim makes the first cut

But maybe, thought one of the men waiting in line, *it's not really nice to get a haircut so close to the Three Weeks? After all, the whole point of not cutting one's hair is as a sign of mourning. Now it looks as if everybody is getting a haircut "in honor" of the days of mourning!*

He decided to share his feelings with R' Chaim Kanievsky and find out if they were correct. It looked as if the whole Jewish world was getting a haircut in honor of the Three Weeks. Was it therefore wrong to have one's hair cut so close to 17 Tammuz?

But R' Chaim did not worry about that at all.

"On the contrary," he said. "We don't get a haircut in honor of the Three Weeks. We get a haircut to honor the halachah, which says that it is forbidden to get a haircut afterward!"

What does a fund-raiser do when he is about to leave the Holy Land to collect *tzedakah*?

A Matter of Trying Why not obtain a *berachah* from one who has the power to give them? After all, he will need a great deal of *siyatta diShmaya* — Heavenly assistance. He wants to succeed in his fund-raising and hopes that people will give *tzedakah* generously.

The fund-raiser went to see R' Chaim Kanievsky to ask for his blessing.

"It doesn't matter how much money you collect," R' Chaim told him. "It's just a matter of *hishtadlus* — of trying. Hashem can send the money from wherever He wants."

Armed with this knowledge, the fund-raiser went on his way. He knew that he was not the one responsible for the success of this campaign. He would try his best, and HaKadosh Baruch Hu would send help from any source He deemed suitable.

When the fund-raiser returned to Eretz Yisrael, he went to see R' Chaim again.

"This is what the Rav told me when I left," he began, repeating R' Chaim's words from his previous visit. "I'd like to relate what I heard on my trip.

"When I was in the United States," the fund-raiser continued, "I met a man who knew why I had come. He told me a story that he had heard from the person it happened to."

This is the story the fund-raiser told:

> When a certain boys' school was founded in Eretz Yisrael, a great deal of money was needed. Not long after the school opened, it ran into financial difficulties. One of the founders traveled to the United States to raise money for the Talmud Torah. To his deep disappointment, the campaign was an outright failure. Wherever he went, he was met with refusals. He was unable to raise the necessary funds.
>
> The fund-raiser returned to Eretz Yisrael, upset and ashamed.
>
> One day, the man was summoned to the Chazon Ish's home. There he was told, to his amazement, that a Jew had come from Australia, bringing $50,000 for the Talmud Torah!
>
> The astonished fund-raiser told the Chazon Ish, "I didn't even go to Australia! This donation has nothing to do with my trip."

"What's the difference where you went?" asked the Chazon Ish. *"You did your hishtadlus. You tried. And Hashem sent the money from some other place."*

"Hashem sent me this story," our fund-raiser told R' Chaim Kanievsky, "as an additional reminder. It only strengthened the lesson the Rav had taught me as I set out to raise funds in America."

The emotional father came to R' Chaim Kanievsky's house together with his son, Yaakov Yisrael. In his hand he held an

All About Names

invitation, fresh off the presses. They were coming to invite the Prince of Torah to the boy's bar mitzvah.

R' Chaim read the invitation and said thoughtfully, as though bringing up a memory, "I saved the boy from being named Yeshurun."

Both the father and the son were very surprised. This was the last thing they'd expected to hear. What did R' Chaim mean? And what did it have to do with Yaakov Yisrael?

"I'll tell you the story," R' Chaim said.

R' Chaim at a *bris*

"Thirteen years ago, when the bar mitzvah boy was born, you came to my father, the Steipler, and asked him to serve as *sandak* at the *bris* that Shabbos. I used to accompany my father to any *bris* where he was honored with being the *sandak*, so we went to this one together. My father was the *sandak*, and I was honored with saying the *berachos*.

"When I said, '*V'yikarei shemo b'Yisrael*' (And his name shall be called in Israel.), you whispered the name Yaakov Yisrael in my ear. This chosen name had, of course, no connection to my father's name, which was also Yaakov Yisrael. You intended to name the baby after your grandfather who'd had that name. But I wasn't sure if I was permitted to say the name in front of my father.

"I was silent for a moment, thinking it over. To remove all doubt, I thought about adding the name Yeshurun, which is very close to Yisrael. In the end, however, I decided that because the name was intended for someone else, there was no problem."

Now the father remembered that, a few days after his son's *bris*, R' Chaim had told him that he'd been uncertain whether or not to say his father's name. But this was the first time he was hearing about the idea of adding on the name Yeshurun. Both father and son were amazed to find that the halachic musings that had passed through R' Chaim's mind thirteen years earlier were still alive in his memory, as though they had taken place that very day!

A yeshivah? Here, in Carmiel? Never!

This was the reaction of the nonreligious Jews living in Carmiel.

Vanishing Opposition

For them, having a yeshivah in their community felt threatening. The yeshivah's influence would be undeniable. But they preferred to be the ones doing the influencing, rather than the ones being influenced.

"Let's make a demonstration!" they decided. "We'll go out into the city streets and show those upstarts who has the *real* power around here!"

And so it happened that, while Yeshivas Orchos Torah was trying to build up Torah in Carmiel, local residents came out in a demonstration against them. But the demonstration was not the only way these people expressed their opposition to the new yeshivah. Some of them sent clear, hostile messages. Others tried to disrupt the project in any way they could.

The yeshivah's administrator, R' Yaakov Virzhvinsky, went to see R' Chaim Kanievsky. He described the work they were doing, and the powerful opposition to it. "There was even a demonstration against us!"

R' Chaim replied, "That is a good sign! When a certain city near Bnei Brak was built, they made a condition that the city would not have a shul. Today, the city has about eight shuls!"

That's how R' Chaim comforted R' Virzhvinsky. "We must not become alarmed by opposition. *B'ezras Hashem*, with time, it will weaken and then disappear."

The homes of our *gedolim* are open to help the public not only at all hours of the day, but also at all hours of the night.

Through the Window

This story teaches that, in such a home, the front door is not the only way to get the answers to our questions. Sometimes you can get them through the window!

It was after midnight in the home of a certain Jewish man. This was a big and important night. Tomorrow morning he would celebrate the *bris* of his newborn son.

Was everything ready for the *bris*? Almost. The big question of what name to give the baby was still being debated.

The husband was upset. His wife was crying. Morning would be here soon. Tension in their home mounted. The baby's father wanted a certain name very badly, but his wife wanted another name just as much.

Finally, with no other option, the man decided to go to R' Chaim Kanievsky's house.

Not many minutes later, the sound of knocking was heard on the window of R' Chaim's apartment. R' Chaim hurried to the window. Who could be knocking so late at night?

"Rebbe!" the man burst out in pain. "I'm so sorry, but this is an emergency!"

He told R' Chaim that his baby's *bris* was to take place in just a few hours, and he still didn't know which name to give him.

"Give him both names," R' Chaim ruled.

And peace returned to the man's home.

A loud, buzzing sound rose from the Kanievsky kitchen. It was the sound of a drill. The family had finally decided that the kitchen

Home Improvement

could no longer remain in its present condition. For years, they had tried to convince the *rebbetzin* to give her permission to improve the kitchen, so that it would look better and be more convenient to work in. But the *rebbetzin*, as always, was firm in her opinion: there was no need for improvements. She was fine with it, just the way it was.

Time passed, leaving its mark on the kitchen. Now there was more of a need than ever to fix up the room. It was finally decided to call someone in to make some minimal improvements.

Three people were in the house: the *rebbetzin*, her son, and the contractor they'd hired to fix up the kitchen. The contractor worked energetically, hammering, drilling ...

The son watched with satisfaction. After so many years, the kitchen would finally be more comfortable. It would also have a much more pleasant look.

And the *rebbetzin*? She cried.

"You should know," she said, "that the gaze of *Klal Yisrael* is focused on the simplicity of this house. Everyone takes an example from it. We must be extra careful about any change we make here."

All the other rooms in the apartment are ordinary rooms — a model of simplicity. The living room is called the "book room." The

"I already have a coat"

The "book room"

room's only adornment is the bookcases full of *sefarim*, which gives the room its name.

"The *sefarim*," the *rebbetzin* declared. "That's the most beautiful decoration of all!"

A Coat for the Mashiach

"Rebbe!" a man told R' Chaim Kanievsky. "I'd like to buy you a new frock coat!" He had come from abroad to visit R' Chaim's home to greet the *tzaddik*.

"I already have a coat for Shabbos, and another one for every day," R' Chaim said.

"But—" The man repeated his request.

"If you want to buy me a coat, then buy one that will be ready to greet Mashiach *tzidkeinu*," R' Chaim said at last.

A great deal of *tzedakah* money passes through the Kanievsky home on its way to needy people. Extra care is taken to make sure

A Secret Gift
that these gifts are given in private, so that those receiving the money won't be embarrassed.

Whenever R' Chaim has *tzedakah* funds to give out, he waits until everyone else has left. He wants to give money to needy people in private. But what can he do? His room has become a public place. People are constantly coming and going.

How to do both things: preserve the dignity of those who receive the *tzedakah*, while not passing up a chance to give?

Rav Chaim gives *tzedakah*

There have been times when R' Chaim has turned to a poor person and said, "I need you." Hearing that R' Chaim wishes to be alone with that person, the others all take their leave. Of course, no one knows the reason R' Chaim wants to talk privately with that person. After everyone else has left the room, R' Chaim closes the door. And only then does he give the money to the person who needs it.

One day, R' Chaim set aside a sum of money for a certain man who was in need of help. R' Chaim began to keep an eye out for him, but for some reason the man did not come to the house. Days passed. One day, R' Chaim spotted the fellow riding in a car down Rashbam Street.

R' Chaim rushed over to the car, which had paused in the traffic. "I have to give you something," R' Chaim told him. But he gave nothing.

The other passengers in the car realized that their presence was not wanted at that moment. The driver pulled over and the others quickly got out of the car.

Only when the two of them were alone in the car, with the door closed and all the other passengers a safe distance away, did R' Chaim give the needy man the envelope of money that he had prepared for him.

The teenager inspected his *tefillin* closely. He was not satisfied with what he saw. There were places on the straps where the black

At Your Service

color was fading. According to the halachah, the black color of the straps should not be faded or peeled.

I must have the color restored as soon as possible, he decided.

He took a bottle of appropriate black dye, spread his *tefillin* on the table, and got ready to begin blackening the straps.

R' Chaim in *tefillin*

Just a minute! He had just thought of a possible problem. Is someone whose beard has not yet begun to grow permitted to blacken the straps of *tefillin*?

He decided to ask R' Chaim Kanievsky.

R' Chaim listened to his question and said, "That is a good question. Bring your *tefillin* here, along with the dye, and I will blacken them."

The next day, that teenager was a hero. His friends listened to his story with interest.

"I want R' Chaim to blacken my *tefillin*, too," someone said.

"Me, too!" added another.

"And me!"

"And me!"

"Let's all go to R' Chaim. We also don't have beards. Let's have him blacken our *tefillin*. What a *zechus*!"

It never crossed the boys' minds that this was not a *zechus*, but an imposition. In their childish desire to win merit, they would be bothering a *gadol hador*.

Eagerly, they inspected the straps of their *tefillin*, searching for areas that needed fixing.

The next day, a full class of boys without beards came to "innocently" ask if they were allowed to blacken their *tefillin*.

R' Chaim understood the real intent behind the question. But he patiently sat and blackened the *tefillin* straps of all the boys in that class.

"How will we live?"

"How will we marry off the children when there is no money?"

Personal Miracles From time to time, anxious fathers come to R' Chaim Kanievsky to share their worries about finding the money they needed to marry off their children.

R' Chaim encourages them and reassures them that Hashem looks out for every single person with special *hashgachah*.

R' Chaim spoke about his own *hashgachah pratis*:

"When my oldest daughter was old enough to get married, my mother undertook to cover a great portion of the financial burden. This was in her later years, when she was not in good health.

"'What will happen later?' she asked. 'How will you marry off the other children?'

"But HaKadosh Baruch Hu, in His kindness and compassion, sent sources of money for each new wedding.

R' Chaim at the wedding of a daughter

"My mother was the miracle for my oldest daughter. After her passing, new miracles appeared with each child who reached marriageable age.

"One year, I was asked to write my comments on the *sefer HaRokeach*. Though they told me they would pay for what I would write, they did not want to talk about money. I spent a full year writing comments on the *sefer* each evening. At the end of the year, I presented my comments, but I did not receive a penny in exchange.

"A month went by, and then two months. A year passed, and then another — and no money. Finally, five years had gone by.

"At the end of those five years, our daughter became engaged. And then, out of the blue, after *five years*, I received payment for that lengthy writing job.

"The money I was paid was the same sum that I had committed myself to paying for the *shidduch* — exactly!"

"There's a problem with the pipe. I have to call the plumber."

The plumber was very happy to come. It was not every day that he was summoned to fix a pipe in such an illustrious home.

The Plumber's Prayer

There are people who stand in line for a long time for a chance to enter R' Chaim Kanievsky's house, while he was invited to come in the moment he arrived. He was expected, and his help was needed. What a privilege! What an amazing *zechus*!

The minute the plumber finished fixing the pipe, R' Chaim came out. Quoting the *pasuk* from the Torah *You shall pay his wages on that same day [that he works for you]*, he paid the plumber on the spot for the repair.

"Tell me," R' Chaim said. "On the *Yamim Nora'im*, when you daven for a livelihood, how do you daven? What do you ask for? Do you request that Jews should have clogged pipes and plumbing problems?"

R' Chaim saying *Tehillim*

The plumber was silent. What should he say? It was true that he earned his living from others' problems.

"Come, let me teach you how to daven for your *parnasah*. You must say: If it has been decreed that someone must suffer, let it not be either physical or spiritual suffering, but only a burst pipe or some such thing. That way, everyone benefits. It's good for them, and it's good for you!"

"We'd like to consult with R' Chaim about a certain appointment," said the men from the Badatz (the Beis Din Tzedek). "We

The Best Advice

would like to appoint Rav So-and-so to be the *rav* of the Badatz, and we want to ask R' Chaim's opinion about it."

"Grab him with both hands!" R' Chaim advised.

They did as he said, and offered the candidate the position of *rav*.

Just a few days later, the candidate himself appeared at the Kanievsky door.

"They've offered me the position of *rav*. I am afraid that the job will interfere with my learning schedule. After all, a *rav* has many responsibilities and interruptions."

"You are right," R' Chaim said. "It's not worth your while to accept the position."

Armed with R' Chaim's agreement, the man turned down the offer.

The men from the Badatz were disappointed. "Perhaps it would be a good idea for you to ask for advice before you decline the position," they suggested.

"I did ask for advice," he said. "I

"I tell every person what's best for him"

R' Chaim listened to the man's fears

asked R' Chaim Kanievsky. I shared my concerns with him. He said that they were valid, and that I should not take the position."

Not long afterward, the delegation came back to R' Chaim.

"Rebbe told us to take him as *rav*. Why, then, did you tell him advice that opposes this?" they wondered.

"I tell every person what will be best for him," R' Chaim said. "For you, it would be best to have him as the *rav*, and that's what I told you. For him, it's better to sit and learn without disturbance, and that's the advice I gave *him*!"

Seventy Books

Nighttime. Everyone was sound asleep and the house was quiet. Suddenly, the silence was shattered by a series of crashes. A pile of books had tumbled out of the bookcase, right onto the bed below!

The head of the household woke up as *sefarim* landed on him. Apparently, the bookshelf above him had collapsed. He tried to extricate himself from the pile of *sefarim* that now decorated his bed.

A strange scenario. And when something strange happens in the dead of night, it seems even stranger.

Why did Hashem do this to me? the man wondered as he kissed each *sefer* and set it in its pile. Is this a hint about something? Why did all the *sifrei kodesh* tumble out of the bookshelf without warning?

The *sefarim* stood in piles on the table. The man began to count them. Ten … twenty … thirty … seventy books in all.

Seventy *sefarim*, in the middle of the night. The strangeness of it all didn't let the man sleep. He decided to describe the incident to R' Chaim Kanievsky. Maybe there was something he was meant to learn from all this. Maybe it was a message from *Shamayim* that he should learn more, or treat his *sefarim* more respectfully.

Worried, the man went to R' Chaim and told him what had happened to him in the middle of the night. Then he described his fears. "Maybe this is a sign that I'm not learning enough?" Maybe it's a sign of this, that, or the other.

R' Chaim listened to the list of the man's fears — and dismissed them. "It's a sign that you have to pick up the *sefarim* and put them back on the bookshelf!" he said.

With a light heart, the man went home to deal with his bookshelf and his *sefarim*.

The results of the blood test didn't please the family doctor. "You'll have to take some more tests," he told the patient, his face **Why Me?** not revealing a thing. Within days, the doctor's fears were realized.

The patient, a *talmid chacham*, was diagnosed with a serious illness.

In distress, the *talmid chacham* turned to his rebbe, the one who guided him in everything: R' Chaim Kanievsky.

"Do not have any treatments, large or small, here in Eretz Yisrael," R' Chaim said firmly. "Only in America! Don't even let them give you an injection in this country."

The patient did as his rebbe had instructed him. He traveled to America, was treated there, and, *baruch Hashem*, recovered from his illness.

Ten years passed. From time to time, the man thought about R' Chaim's advice. Over the course of time, he'd heard about other people who were diagnosed with the same illness. But, unlike him, when they came to consult with R' Chaim he had told them to go ahead and have treatments done in Eretz Yisrael.

And even before he'd fallen ill, he had heard about patients who consulted with R' Chaim and were told to use a hospital right here at home.

The question would not leave his mind. Why had R' Chaim given him the opposite advice?

The next time I see the doctor, he decided, *I'll ask him what he thinks about this story.*

"When, exactly, did this happen?" the doctor wanted to know.

The patient thought back and gave the doctor the exact date, ten years earlier, when he had gone to speak to R' Chaim Kanievsky about his illness.

"That's amazing," the doctor exclaimed. "At that exact time, a new form of treatment was discovered in America — a treatment not known anywhere else in the world. Had you received as much as a single injection here in Eretz Yisrael, they would not have been able to use the new treatment on you.

"Subsequently, when the treatment was seen to be successful, it spread to the rest of the world, including here in our own country.

"But how did your *rav* know about the new treatment?" the doctor wondered. "Someone must have told him about it."

The patient agreed: R' Chaim *had* known about the new treatment. But no person had told him about this breakthrough in the field of medicine. R' Chaim sat in his room and learned all day. He had learned about it straight from *Shamayim*.

The man decided to tell R' Chaim what he'd just heard from the doctor.

"I received wonderfully precise advice," he marveled. "Advice that patients who came before me could not have used, and that patients after me did not need!"

R' Chaim, in his humility, did not lend much weight to the story. "I just figured that here in Eretz Yisrael they know nothing, but there, in America, at least they know a little."

"Yes, but those who came before me received different advice," the man insisted.

"Oh, well," R' Chaim murmured. "It all came from *Shamayim*."

Yes, it had all come from *Shamayim*. As the *pasuk* says, *Hashem shares His secrets with those who fear Him!* (*Tehillim* 25:14).

Opening a new institution calls for enormous sums of money. But anyone who has ever tried to open one knows that money is not

What's in a Name? enough. Such an undertaking calls for enormous human resources as well: people who are willing to pour their hearts and minds into the new place; people eager to give of their talent and their time; people ready to undertake any job at all, with a full heart.

A certain institution like this had two such people.

One of them donated money to the place very generously.

The other was a woman who poured all her energy into the new institution. She was Rebbetzin Batsheva Kanievsky, a"h.

Sadly, by the time the place actually opened, Rebbetzin Batsheva was no longer among the living.

The donor, who knew about the *rebbetzin's* extraordinary help to the institution, suggested that they put her name on the building. He could have had the name of one of his own relatives there, but he wanted to put Rebbetzin Kanievsky's name there instead.

The director of the institution decided to ask R' Chaim Kanievsky for his opinion in this matter.

"Would the *rebbetzin's neshamah* receive an *aliyah*, an elevation, from having her name on the building?" the director asked.

R' Chaim replied, "You can name the building after the *rebbetzin*, but I don't know if there is a merit in such a thing. It doesn't matter what a building is called. *Shamayim* knows the truth.

"The only point in its favor is that, seeing her name there, others may be inspired to help such institutions as well. Causing others to support Torah institutions — there is certainly an elevation for the *neshamah* in that!"

Oh no! This was terrible! The devoted parents could hardly believe the bad news they'd just heard.

The Operation That Wasn't

Their daughter was getting older and in sore need of a *shidduch*. The parents had searched and searched for one, until this new blow struck. Their worry over a *shidduch* fell away in the face of this new fear. Their daughter was quickly given a series of treatments, but her condition only grew worse. Finally, with her life in danger, the doctors decided that she needed to have an operation — immediately!

The girl went to the Kanievsky home and poured out her heart to the Rebbetzin, who went to speak to R' Chaim.

"She should support Torah," R' Chaim urged. "In that merit, she will be healed.

"But," he added, "she shouldn't just give *tzedakah*. She must support the Torah!"

The young woman, who had money, decided to support a *kollel*.

A week passed. The patient flew abroad and was admitted to a hospital. Now she was lying on the operating table.

The surgery began, and the doctors could not believe their eyes. Over and over, they compared what they were seeing to the worrisome scans of the patient's body. To their astonishment, the growth that had been making the young woman ill seemed to have disappeared! There was no longer any need for an operation.

When they told this story to R' Aharon Leib Shteinman, he said, "The merit of supporting Torah saved her. The Torah can do anything!"

For days, the yeshivah's financial director was beside himself. Today he must pay a large debt. He must repay 120,000 shekels to the

A Great Blessing

person from whom the yeshivah had borrowed it, and the money was simply not to be found! He had no idea whom he could turn to for help.

At last, in desperation, he decided to go to R' Chaim Kanievsky and ask for a *berachah*.

The director told R' Chaim about the yeshivah's dire financial straits. R' Chaim listened to what he said and gave him a *berachah*.

But the director wasn't satisfied.

"Rebbe," he pleaded, "I need a *big berachah*!"

"May you have a *big berachah*!" R' Chaim said warmly.

The director left the Kanievsky home and started back for the yeshivah.

"*Shalom aleichem!*" a man greeted him. He was the father of one of the yeshivah's students.

"Tell me," the man continued, "do you perhaps need a loan? I am able to give the yeshivah a loan of 120,000 shekels. You can pay it back in installments."

The financial director was dumbfounded. Right before his eyes, the *berachah* that R' Chaim Kanievsky had given him just a few minutes before had come true!

He felt a powerful need to tell R' Chaim about the miracle that had just occurred.

R' Chaim reacted the way he so often did, when seeing the outcome of his *berachos* and advice. "It's all from *Shamayim*."

R' Chaim Walkin, *shlita*, came to R' Chaim Kanievsky together with another man. He introduced his companion, who was from

Why Gibraltar?

Gibraltar.

"Oh, you're from Gibraltar?" R' Chaim asked in excitement.

When asked why he was so excited about meeting someone from Gibraltar, R' Chaim replied, "The halachah is that when one sees *HaYam HaGadol* — 'The Great Sea' — one makes a special *berachah*, '*Oseh HaYam HaGadol*' — 'Who makes the Great Sea.' But there is a disagreement among *poskim* which sea this refers to: the Mediterranean Sea or the Atlantic Ocean.

"Because the answer is uncertain, we just make the *berachah* of *Oseh ma'aseh bereishis* — 'He Who makes all of Creation' when seeing these seas.

"But Gibraltar is located at the meeting point between these two great bodies of water, and you can see both of them at the same time. So when one is in Gibraltar one can make the *berachah* according to all opinions."

It was parent-teacher conference night. Little Dovid's father walked hesitantly through the door. He was afraid to speak to

Who Is the Doctor?

his son's rebbi. His young son was having a very hard time at school. All his classmates already knew how to read, while Dovid had been left behind.

The door kept opening and closing as fathers went in and out. They entered calmly and left looking happy.

And he? Ah … there are some fathers who have been blessed with the riches of having successful children. Hashem had blessed *him* with plenty of money. He was a very wealthy man. *But what will be with my son?*

The man decided to go see R' Chaim Kanievsky.

"I heard that a certain *talmid chacham* is interested in publishing his original Torah thoughts. I am prepared to give half the money it costs to publish the *sefer*. In exchange, I want to ask for salvation for my young son. He has a problem reading."

"It will be all right!" R' Chaim replied.

The man donated half the sum needed to publish the *sefer*.

After the Pesach break, the phone rang in the rich man's house.

"This is your son's teacher," the rebbe said. "I want to know which doctor or psychologist you took your son to. *Baruch* Hashem, his problem has completely disappeared. The boy reads fluently now."

As soon as he had hung up with the teacher, the father made another phone call — to the *talmid chacham* who was putting out his *sefer*.

"I am going to donate the rest of the money that you need to publish!" he cried happily.

The doctors stood around the sick woman, very worried. There was some sort of serious infection in her body. She must have an

Better to Do Nothing

operation at once! If not, her life was at risk.

The patient's family rushed a letter to R' Chaim Kanievsky, asking him what to do. Was it advisable to find an expert on infections? they asked. Maybe such an expert would be able to solve the problem.

R' Chaim read the note and said, "Daven!"

"But the doctors say that without an operation her life is in danger," the family protested. "According to them, she might die!"

"Daven, and she won't die!" came the clear answer.

Armed with R' Chaim's advice, the family firmly opposed the proposed surgery.

Not long afterward, the doctor examined the sick woman again. This time, he changed his opinion entirely.

"If we operate, her life will be at risk," the doctor declared, though he did not change his opinion that *without* an operation her life was also in danger!

Once again, messengers were rushed to R' Chaim with the doctor's words.

"It is preferable to sit and do nothing," R' Chaim ruled.

Indeed, the patient was treated without surgery. The treatment was successful, and she was no longer in danger.

With wisdom and pleasant manners...

"There's a big *talmid chacham* waiting to see you," R' Chaim Kanievsky was told. A few minutes later, the man was seated in front of R' Chaim.

Good Manners

If the fellow was a *talmid chacham*, there was nothing more natural for R' Chaim than to talk Torah with him. The moment the man entered, R' Chaim asked him a question in learning. To his distress, the other man didn't know how to answer him.

The *kollel* man began to tell R' Chaim about the problem that he had come to discuss.

"My situation," he said, "disturbs me very much and makes it hard for me to concentrate on my learning."

R' Chaim felt badly that he had distressed him earlier with his question. Smiling warmly, he said, "So *that's* why you couldn't remember the answer to my question!"

With wisdom and pleasant manners, R' Chaim smoothed over the unpleasantness that had happened when his visitor walked in.

The *gaon* R' Yitzchak Zilberstein, *shlita*, tells the following story: With a heavy heart, the sick Jew went to see the *gadol* R' Chaim Kanievsky. A terrible disease had attacked his body. *I will go to R' Chaim for a berachah for a speedy recovery*, he thought.

Above Nature

"What must I do in order to be saved from this terrible sickness?" he asked R' Chaim.

"To be saved from the situation you're in is not within the laws of nature. In that case, you must do something unnatural. When you behave in a way that's not natural, then *Shamayim* will treat you measure for measure and heal you in a way that's not natural and, *b'ezras Hashem*, you will see salvation."

"What does the Rav call 'unnatural'?" the patient wanted to know. "What must I do?"

"You tell me," R' Chaim said. "Do you have impure devices that have been forbidden by the *gedolei hador*?"

The sick man was forced to admit that, to his shame, he did own such devices.

"If you break your dependency on those things, which has become second nature to you by now, you will be healed! You must abandon these devices and get them out of your house. Then you will be healed of your illness."

R' Chaim's words touched the patient's heart. He removed the devices from his home and from his heart; he threw them out of the house!

"I can testify," concludes R' Zilberstein, "that just as R' Chaim said, the man was healed in a way that rose above the laws of nature!"

Rebbetzin Kanievsky was known for being a good listener and for sharing in the sorrows of Jewish girls. She was noted for her *berachos* and her *tefillos* to save people from difficult situations.

Not the Cure, but the Blessing

Every day, many women and girls came to her home, each one burdened by her own packet of troubles and questions, each one looking for advice and guidance in both material and spiritual matters.

Among them was a woman with ailing kidneys.

"Grind up a watermelon and drink the juice," the *rebbetzin* advised her. "Watermelon juice will help with your kidney problem."

The woman did as the *rebbetzin* suggested. From that day on, she made it a practice of drinking watermelon juice for her health. And, *baruch Hashem*, she saw good results.

Time passed. The righteous *rebbetzin* passed from this world.

That woman cried, like so many others whom the *rebbetzin* had helped with her good advice and blessings. The woman was grateful that the *rebbetzin* had given her such good medical advice. Every time she felt ill with kidney disease, she would drink watermelon juice and her symptoms would vanish.

The next time she had an attack, she prepared the watermelon juice as usual, just the way the *rebbetzin* had taught her. But what was going on? This time the juice did not help at all.

When R' Chaim Kanievsky heard this story, he said, "The patient thinks that it was the treatment that helped, that watermelon juice has medical powers. That's not the case. It was not the medicine that healed her, but the *rebbetzin's berachah*. Now that she's gone, so is the blessing."

CHAPTER 4
The Lederman Shul

The Lederman Shul on Rashbam Street. The shul where R' Chaim's father, the Steipler Gaon, *zt"l*, used to daven. The shul where today many will go to daven so that they can pray in the same *minyan* as R' Chaim himself. The Steipler used to have a special place near the *mizrach vant* (eastern wall) of the Lederman Shul. R' Chaim did not sit near him. Instead, he sat near the *bimah* in the center of the shul. The man seated beside the Steipler was R' Aharon Honigsberg, who assisted him in his last years during davening.

Fear of Judgment

Rav Chaim in his *kittel*

One Yom Kippur, when it was time for *Ne'ilah*, R' Chaim went over to stand and daven next to his father. The other men in the shul were surprised.

Later, R' Honigsberg went to R' Chaim and asked him, respectfully, why he saw fit to change his place during *Ne'ilah*.

R' Chaim answered, "I was afraid to be alone during *Ne'ilah*, so I went to stand next to my father."

What should we feel if R' Chaim himself felt afraid on the Day of Atonement?

A new year had arrived — a year of fresh hopes and dreams. The custom among Jewish people everywhere is to wish each other a good year on Rosh Hashanah night.

For a Good Year

On this night of Rosh Hashanah, davening was long over, but not the exchange of good wishes. Many, many people wanted to receive a *berachah* from a *tzaddik* on this special day. Why not go to the Prince of Torah, R' Chaim Kanievsky, to receive his blessing for the new year?

The streets were packed. Many people — thousands in number — streamed to the Lederman Shul to receive R' Chaim's *berachah* for a *shanah tovah*, a good year.

Giving, and getting, *berachos*

An hour passed. Then two, and three. The line grew shorter and longer at the same steady pace. Each man with his needs, each man with his *berachah*. As custom dictates, those who received a blessing also gave one in their turn, which stretched the whole proceedings to double the length of time.

Hour followed hour. R' Chaim's strength was waning as the number of people receiving his *berachah* increased.

Maybe, those close to him murmured, it was time to put an end to this custom. After all, the *rav* was so weak.

But R' Chaim was firm. He would continue the custom. "Is it possible to pass up on *berachos*?" he said. "So many Jews bless me to have a good year. Do you think giving those blessings up is a small thing?"

"I'd like to see R' Chaim Kanievsky and ask him for a *berachah*." This request repeats itself day after day, in the scores and in the **Blessings** hundreds. Who would not want to receive a *berachah* from R' Chaim Kanievsky, the Prince of Torah?

Everyone appreciates the value of his *berachos*. Some travel long distances and give up a lot of their time, simply to bask in a *berachah* from that great *tzaddik*. And everyone is happy when they get such a blessing, because they believe that it will come true.

Apparently, R' Chaim himself shares that belief — not necessarily in his own *berachos*, but in the *berachos* of others.

It was the first night of Rosh Hashanah, and davening had been over for some time. This was the chance for the people in shul to have the awesome privilege of receiving a blessing for a good new year from R' Chaim Kanievsky: "May you be inscribed for a good year."

To bless and to be blessed.

When R' Chaim returned home, he told his wife, the *rebbetzin*, "This year will surely be a good one for us. So many Jews have given me a *berachah*."

"This year I'm going to daven in Bnei Brak on Rosh Hashanah," a certain *ba'al teshuvah* resolved. "This year I will daven in the same minyan as R' Chaim Kanievsky!"

A Dream Come True

The *ba'al teshuvah* had come a long way, and he knew that he still had a great deal of work to do. He would continue learning and strengthen himself along the proper road. Now, with the *Yamim Nora'im* approaching, he had a powerful urge to daven in the Lederman Shul on Rosh Hashanah—the shul where R' Chaim davened. But where would he eat and sleep while he was in Bnei Brak?

I will rent a room in a Bnei Brak hotel, he decided. And so he did.

On the first night of Rosh Hashanah, his dream came true. He was sitting in the Lederman Shul. At any moment davening would begin: Rosh Hashanah *Ma'ariv* with the Prince of Torah!

After davening, the man approached R' Chaim to ask for a *berachah*. But, apart from that, he also needed some practical guidance. That year the first day of Rosh Hashanah was also Shabbos, when we eat three meals and wash over *lechem mishneh*, two loaves of challah.

"I have only one loaf in my room," the man told R' Chaim. "What should I do? Must I bring over another loaf, so that I'll have *lechem*

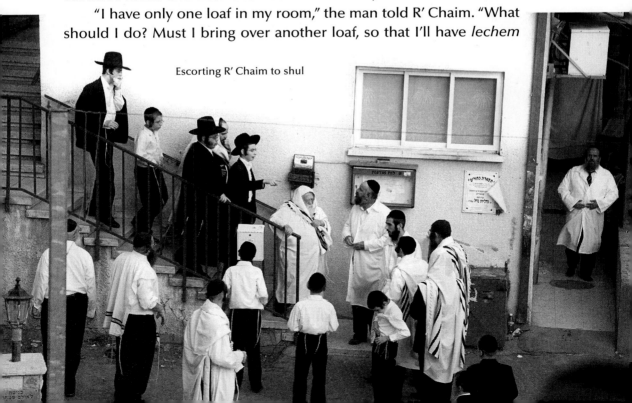

Escorting R' Chaim to shul

mishneh, or can I use one loaf alone? Or maybe there's a third option that I'm not aware of?"

R' Chaim had an instant solution to the fellow's problem. "You will be my guest! You're going to eat all three Shabbos meals in my home."

Together they walked out of the shul toward the Kanievsky house, where the man was welcomed with honor. R' Chaim made sure that his guest was comfortable and lacked for nothing.

The man's joy was boundless. He had hoped only to daven near R' Chaim — and had ended up eating all three meals on Shabbos Rosh Hashanah at R' Chaim's own table!

The men who davened in the same *minyan* as R' Chaim Kanievsky, at the Lederman Shul, can

On His Feet

testify how hard he worked never to fall asleep outside the succah.

It was Shabbos Chol HaMo'ed in the year 2012, and R' Chaim felt tired and weak. What does a man of advanced years do when he is exhausted? He tries to sit comfortably, in a way that will allow him to rest.

R' Chaim in the succah

But R' Chaim operated in a completely different way. Feeling weak and tired, he decided to stand up!

The other men in shul were astounded to see him rise to his feet and remain standing during the entire reading of *Megillas Koheles*, just to keep himself from falling asleep outside the succah.

It was a Monday morning *Shacharis* in the Lederman Shul. When they reached the Torah reading, the *gabbai* became emotional. The

Rav Chaim Refuses man he called up to the Torah had his *aliyah*, and then they made a *"Mi SheBeirach"* for him … and for his wife, who had just given birth … and for their newborn daughter. The baby's name was called out, and finally, "May her father and mother merit raising her to Torah, *chuppah*, and good deeds, amen!"

"Mazel tov!" everyone called out to the happy young man.

After davening, the new father went over to R' Chaim Kanievsky and asked, "Does the *rav* remember me?"

"No," R' Chaim replied. "I don't."

"I was at your house a year ago …" And he related the story.

One year before, the young man had knocked on the Kanievsky door.

"Tomorrow, my wife and I will be traveling out of the country," he said, heartbroken. "We've been married five years already, and we are still childless. We're flying to another country tomorrow to undergo a certain treatment to help us have a child." After telling his tale, he requested a *berachah* from R' Chaim.

"No, I cannot bless you," R' Chaim said. "I know that my father, the Steipler, *zt"l*, did not feel comfortable about this sort of treatment. Therefore, I cannot give you a *berachah* for its success."

"Rebbe!" the young man pleaded. "I didn't come here for a halachic ruling. I came for a *berachah*!"

But R' Chaim was adamant. "I cannot give you one."

When the young man saw that R' Chaim would not change his mind, he didn't know what to do.

"What will I tell my wife? She is so sad. How will I come back empty-handed?"

"Look," R' Chaim said, "if you don't make the trip, Hashem will help!"

"Of course," the new father said happily, "we did as the *rav* suggested. We canceled the trip and the treatment. And Hashem helped us! Only a year has passed since that day and, *baruch Hashem*, we have been blessed with a daughter!"

"A good question … a good question," the boy heard.

In that case, he thought, *if it's such a good question, I'll take it to R' Chaim Kanievsky!*

Ask, My Son

Yes, he decided. *On motza'ei Shabbos, during the short break before Ma'ariv. I'll ask him then.*

Impatiently he waited for his big moment. Over and over he rehearsed his question so that he'd be able to say it clearly.

With the children

When the moment came, the boy stood among all the men waiting their turn to speak with R' Chaim. The line moved forward. Soon it would be his turn. He reviewed his question one last time, his heart pounding with excitement.

But, what was this? An adult man pushed him aside, moving him out of his place in the line and pressing forward to ask a question of his own. When the man was finished, the chazzan's voice rang out with the first words of *Ma'ariv*. The boy's chance was lost.

Disappointed, he went back to his seat to daven.

A bitter taste filled his mouth. It was the taste of disappointment. When davening was over, the boy got ready to leave the shul together with a group of other boys who had davened in the same *minyan*.

Suddenly, to his astonishment, he saw R' Chaim standing among the boys and looking directly at him with a fatherly gaze.

R' Chaim had noticed what had happened in the line earlier. The minute *Ma'ariv* was finished, he went over to the young boy and inquired, "What did you want to ask?"

Respect for Sefarim

The *gabbaim* in the Lederman Shul looked over the bookcase, where dozens of Gemaras were arranged on the shelves. Long years of use had left their mark: here a tattered binding, there pages falling out. And the same was true of the bookcase holding the siddurim.

Now a decision had to be made: what to do? Repair the *sefarim* or buy new ones?

Usually, when it comes to shuls, people are inclined to buy new. It's a way of honoring Hashem, and it's easier to learn and daven from new *sefarim*.

And then there is the money consideration. When the prices were checked, it turned out that the cost of repairing and rebinding a volume was more expensive than buying a new one.

But the *gabbaim* decided not to make the decision by themselves. Instead, they turned to R' Chaim Kanievsky and asked him what they should do. Fix or buy?

"It's a humiliation to *sefarim* to put them in a *genizah*," R' Chaim said. "Siddurim and *sefarim* are meant to be used, not stored away in a *genizah*. That's how we honor them. It's better to repair them and not buy new ones."

Anyone who's ever been with R' Chaim knows how careful he is to treat *sefarim* with respect. Every scrap of paper from a *sefer* or its cover is treated with honor.

Once, a small piece of brown paper, used as the wrapper of a *Mishnah Berurah*, was found clinging to his coat. R' Chaim was about to leave the room when he suddenly noticed the scrap of the book cover on his clothes.

"*Genizah!*" R' Chaim called out. He turned around and went back to put the scrap of paper in a special envelope for safekeeping, so that it could be stored with honor.

It was a usual sight to see R' Chaim taking the trouble, at his advanced age, to get up from his seat in order to rearrange a holy book lying facedown on a pile of *sefarim*. He did it so that those present would understand how serious this

The Lederman Shul

On his way home from shul

is, and to teach them to do the same: "to avoid having the head down and the feet on top!"

When someone once brought him a new *sefer,* on which there were verses from the Torah printed on the cover, R' Chaim told the author that *pesukim* should not be used to decorate a book cover. The next time he put out a book, R' Chaim said, he should avoid doing so again.

Friday night. Davening had just finished in the Lederman Shul. But this Shabbos, unlike other weeks, everyone stayed in his place.

Be Careful What You Say This Shabbos had been designated as a time for strengthening themselves in matters of kashrus. It had been decided that every shul in Bnei Brak would have a *talmid chacham* speak on the subject.

In the Lederman Shul, too, a *talmid chacham* got up to speak.

When he finished speaking, R' Chaim Kanievsky turned to him and said, "*Yasher ko'ach!*" Thank you!

"For what?" the speaker asked in jest. "For keeping my speech short?"

"No," R' Chaim said. "Thank you for speaking words of *chizuk* about kashrus, and not speaking out against any kashrus organization."

A rare mitzvah

There are many mitzvos written in the Torah that are not practiced today. Others *are* still practiced, but the opportunities to do them are rare. R' Chaim Kanievsky took the trouble to run after rare mitzvos that do not come up in everyday life. He did this in order to achieve spiritual perfection, because every mitzvah that we do helps to perfect a person spiritually.

A *Sefer Torah* for the Shul

Some of the mitzvos that R' Chaim ran after were the mitzvah of *peter pidyon chamor*, redeeming a firstborn donkey (by giving a Kohen a lamb or kid in its stead, or paying the value of the donkey), and *reishis hageiz* (giving a Kohen the first cuttings of wool shorn from a sheep raised in Eretz Yisrael).

With the same goal in mind, R' Chaim began writing a *sefer Torah*, which is an explicit mitzvah in the Torah. Though the writing was spread out over a number of years, no one but the *rebbetzin* knew about it. R' Chaim wrote the *sefer Torah* modestly, without fanfare, and even when the time came to bring it into the shul, he did not publicize his mitzvah.

Only on the last day did R' Chaim tell the rest of his family his secret. On *motza'ei Shabbos*, the *sefer Torah* was brought down to the Lederman Shul in a quiet, modest way. Only two candles were burning, as a very small contingent of family members accompanied the new *sefer Torah* to its home in the shul.

In recent years, R' Chaim Kanievsky started davening in a special *minyan* in his home every day. Weakness made it hard for him to go

The Bridge of Halachah

down to the shul next door and then back up to his apartment again.

The shul's *gabbaim* undertook to build a bridge leading from the door of his house straight to a special door they put in at the side of the shul. Then the shul's second floor would run parallel to his house in a straight line. This way, the *gabbaim* thought, it would be easy for R' Chaim to go to shul, and many people could continue davening in the same *minyan* as him.

But R' Chaim looks at everything through the eyes of the Torah. When he was asked to daven in the shul by using the bridge, he mentioned a halachah in the *Shulchan Aruch* that says that

A bridge to shul

one should enter a shul through one door and leave through another. In that case, though he could enter via the bridge, he would have to leave through a different door — using the stairs, which would be too hard for his strength.

No one had thought of this. But the *gabbaim* did not give up. With special artistry, they arranged for *two* doors to the shul to stand side by side at the end of the bridge — one for going in and the other for going out.

R' Chaim also reminded them to make the doors in such a way that the mitzvah of mezuzah could be done. *Baruch Hashem*, everything was carried out to his satisfaction. R' Chaim could now use the bridge to daven in shul along with everyone else. As it says (*Mishlei* 14:28), *B'rov am hadras melech* — "The splendor of a king is seen through the multitudes of his subjects [davening together]!"

CHAPTER 5
The "Prince" of Torah

About 20 years ago, R' Chaim Kanievsky was asked to participate in the *chuppah* of the son of R' Avraham Yosef Shapiro, *z"l*. When he arrived at the wedding hall, R' Chaim found the *chuppah* already in place outdoors. He took a chair, placed it under the *chuppah*, and sat down to learn.

Chasan Torah

Meanwhile, the family members, relatives, and guests arrived. The band came and a crowd gathered. Everyone who entered the hall had the privilege of seeing a rare and precious spectacle: R' Chaim Kanievsky sitting and learning Gemara in total absorption.

When it was time for the *chuppah*, the *chasan* and his escorts approached to the strains of music, with the throng following behind. But the *chuppah* was still occupied...

R' Chaim did not notice what was happening.

"Rebbe," one of the men called. But R' Chaim was lost in a different world.

The man touched the *tzaddik's* arm and added, "Rebbe, it's time for the *chuppah*."

It was only then that the *Chasan Torah* stepped out from under the *chuppah* to let the happy *chasan* take his place.

It was 3:05 a.m. Suddenly there was the sound of knocking on the front door.

Midnight Chavrusa

A knock? At such an hour? *Who could it be*? the household wondered.

And then they remembered.

This was no dangerous or unusual occurrence. *Baruch Hashem*, this happened every so often. And what it meant was…

The head of the household hurried to the door as fast as he could. Oh no! If R' Chaim Kanievsky was knocking, it meant that he was late.

Indeed, he saw that their learning partnership was supposed to have started five minutes before. He had found it difficult to shake off the shreds of sleep, and so he was late.

Now he was ready, as he'd been the day before and the day before that.

And then he sat down, as he did each day, to learn *Seder Zera'im* with the Prince of Torah at 3 o'clock in the morning.

Their learning *seder* always began at precisely 3 a.m. If the hands of the clock ever moved past the 12 — even just five minutes past the hour — R' Chaim would go to his *chavrusa's* door and knock on it to wake him up.

Once, as they sat learning while the world around them slept, there was a power outage. What to do? How could they learn with the whole house plunged in darkness?

But the learning continued unabated, the *chavrusa* reported. R' Chaim quoted the commentary of the Rosh fluently, from memory, word for word.

"Rebbe," R' Elazar Tzaddok Turchin told R' Chaim Kanievsky, "there is no index (a list of topics) in my *Mishnah Berurah*. I need an index!"

A Unique Key

On the spot, R' Chaim took a sheet of paper and wrote down the index to the *Mishnah Berurah* for him.

R' Turchin was stunned. He had complained about needing an index, but had never thought that *this* would be the solution!

When R' Chaim was done, R' Turchin took the index, written in R' Chaim's own writing, and compared it to the printed index in a volume of the *Mishnah Berurah*. And he saw that it exactly corresponded to the one he had just received.

The future *chasan* listened in astonishment to the messenger's words.

You Can Still Change Your Mind...

The wedding was scheduled for the next day. Tomorrow he would have the privilege of joining R' Chaim Kanievsky's illustrious family. Becoming R' Chaim's son-in-law was a tremendous honor!

This was the way the *chasan* felt. His father-in-law, apparently, felt the exact opposite.

Writing *chiddushei Torah*

The messenger announced, "The *kallah's* father, HaGaon R' Chaim Kanievsky, sent me to tell you that his daughter, the *kallah*, is left-handed."

The Gemara says that any kind of physical blemish or flaw disqualifies a Kohen from serving in the Beis HaMikdash. The same blemishes can also serve as grounds for nullifying an engagement. Being left-handed is one of the things that can disqualify a Kohen.

Until that day, R' Chaim had forgotten to inform the *chasan* about this technical "flaw" in his daughter. He sent a messenger to tell him about it now — and to give the young man a chance to change his mind if he wished.

(Which, of course, he didn't!)

Rosh Hashanah. It was the year that R' Chaim Kanievsky's daughter became engaged to the son of R' Aharon Leib Shteinman, *shlita*.

On Second Thought... *I'll go over to R' Aharon Leib to wish him a good Yom Tov*, R' Chaim decided. The thought turned into action, and he set out at once.

Suddenly, halfway there, he stopped walking.

No. He changed his mind. *If I go to R' Aharon Leib now, then on another Yom Tov R' Aharon Leib will feel obligated to come to me. I mustn't put him to any trouble.*

R' Elyashiv and R' Chaim at a wedding *seudah*

The *mechutanim*

So he turned around and retraced his steps, setting aside his plan to walk over to his *mechutan* to wish him a good year.

Many years after the Chazon Ish left this world, the granddaughter of R' Chaim's sister, Rebbetzin Barzam, got married. The wedding

Putting Off the *Simchah* took place during the week of the Chazon Ish's *yahrzeit*. On the night of the *yahrzeit*, a *sheva berachos* was scheduled to take place in the Barzam home.

"Is it proper for me to make a *sheva berachos* in my house on the Chazon Ish's *yahrzeit*?" Rebbetzin Barzam asked her brother, R' Chaim Kanievsky.

"Is that the last night you can make *sheva berachos*?" R' Chaim asked. "If not, it is preferable to put off the *simchah* to another night."

Family members were surprised at this ruling. Why? She was not the Chazon Ish's daughter. Why did she have to be careful not to make a *simchah* on his *yahrtzeit*?

"We grew up like his own children," R' Chaim told them. "Though it is not forbidden by halachah, it wouldn't be proper."

Although all eyes turn to R' Chaim Kanievsky to learn the halachah, when it comes to special added practices that he takes

Washing Hands

upon himself, he is willing to bow to another's opinion.

Many fathers bring their 3-year-old sons to the Kanievsky home to have R' Chaim snip off a bit of their hair before they get their first haircut. For many years, R' Chaim would not wash his hands after cutting such hair, based on a statement in the Gemara *Pesachim*. However, he later heard that R' Aharon Leib Shteinman *is* careful to wash his hands after cutting a child's hair.

Ever since then, R' Chaim, too, began to take on this stringency, even though he believes there is no need to do so.

Washing his hands

Gedolim show respect to every Jew, old and young

Many people run after honor, but there is just one tried-and-true recipe for success.

Who Is Honored? Many believe that only by trampling on other people and acting like they are better can they receive honor, but they're wrong. Chazal have taught that the road to honor comes from completely humbling oneself in order to honor other people.

Our *gedolim*, great as they are, show respect to every Jew, old and young.

One Shabbos, a number of yeshivah boys were guests at R' Chaim's table. When the *seudah* was over and *bentchers* were passed around, one of the guests did not receive one.

R' Chaim, at his advanced age, personally stood up to bring that *bachur* a *bentcher*.

"Is Rebbe so scrupulous about *bentching* from a *bentcher*?" asked someone who was present.

"I thought that *bachur* might feel insulted that he was the only one who didn't get a *bentcher*," R' Chaim explained. "So I stood up to get him one."

R' Michel Yehuda and R' Chaim

In Shevat, in the year 5760 (2000), the *rosh yeshivah* of the Ponevezh *yeshivah ketanah*, R' Michel Yehuda Lefkowitz, was asked

Listening to Our Sages

to serve as *sandak* at the bris of twin boys. R' Chaim Kanievsky was asked to serve as the first *sandak* at precisely 2 p.m., followed by R' Lefkowitz at 2:15 p.m. — after *Minchah* in the yeshivah — for the second boy.

The *mohel* arrived late. He was getting ready to give the first baby a bris milah when R' Lefkowitz entered the hall ready to serve as *sandak* for the second baby. Out of respect for his rebbi, R' Chaim refused to act as the first baby's *sandak* before R' Lefkowitz. (R' Lefkowitz had been the head of Yeshivas Tiferes Tzion, attended by R' Chaim, before becoming *rosh yeshivah* in Ponevezh.) R' Lefkowitz, however, refused to serve before R' Chaim!

They pleaded with R' Lefkowitz to change his mind. He finally approached R' Chaim and said, "I am about to fulfill the mitzvah of listening to the words of our sages," meaning that he was listening to Rav Chaim and going first.

And then he stepped up to serve as *sandak*.

Even in the hospital,
no break from learning

No rest, even when
R' Chaim is hospitalized

In the year 5762 (2002), R' Chaim Kanievsky fell ill and was admitted to the hospital. One day while he was there, a doctor asked

Hospital Talk

him, "When do you think you'll be ready to go home?" This is a question that many patients answer in the same way: "As soon as I can manage on my own." But how, exactly, do they define the word *manage*? What is the minimum that's necessary for a patient to be able to "manage" at home?

When R' Chaim was asked this question, he told the doctor, "When I can take a *sefer* down from the bookcase." This was the minimum "managing" that R' Chaim considered necessary for a Torah-learning Jew!

On another occasion, when he was once again in the hospital for tests, the doctor came to his room and explained R' Chaim's medical condition. When he was done, the doctor asked, "Does the *rav* have any questions?"

"Yes," R' Chaim said promptly. "In Torah!"

R' Chaim Kanievsky was admitted to Mayanei HaYeshua Hospital. He was terribly weak. But despite his illness, and despite his

Honor *Talmidei Chachamim*

weakness, R' Chaim gathered the strength to perform an important mitzvah.

The *gaon* R' Yehudah Shapiro, *zt"l*, was hospitalized in the same hospital at the same time as R' Chaim. "I would like to visit R' Yehudah Shapiro," R' Chaim said.

The plan was not an easy one. It involved great effort for R' Chaim. With difficulty he struggled to put on his coat and hat in honor of the *talmid chacham* he was about to visit. And then he went down to the floor below to pay him a visit and accord him the honor that a *talmid chacham* deserves!

A member of the Kanievsky family related, "I once went to R' Chaim's house, since he needed my help with something. For some

The Delay

reason, he wouldn't let me help him right away. He seemed to be waiting for something.

"'Why are we waiting?' I asked.

"R' Chaim's answer astounded me. 'Your children are here in the room. They are supposed to show you respect. It's not appropriate for them to see their father serving me.'"

One winter Shabbos a number of years ago, the gas under the *blech* went out at the start of the night. The next day, the cholent

Cold Cholent

was cold.

That Shabbos, R' Chaim ate more than his usual amount of cholent, in order not to cause his wife distress over serving him cold food.

R' Elyashiv and R' Chaim

R' Yosef Shalom Elyashiv, the father-in-law of R' Chaim Kanievsky, was an extraordinary *masmid*. Even when he was very old, weak, and frail, he learned Torah with all his might.

Those Who Toil in Torah

When people expressed their amazement over this, R' Chaim would tell them, "If someone forms the habit of learning Torah with exceptional diligence all his life, Hashem helps him over and above the laws of nature.

"The *Talmud Yerushalmi* says that after the age of 80 people have a difficult time with their health — a reality that can't be escaped. But despite his medical situation, a Jew who accustomed himself to learning with complete devotion receives special treatment even when times are hard."

One year, R' Chaim needed to see a doctor on Chanukah. While R' Yoel, the doctor, took an interest in R' Chaim's physical health,

Miraculous Chanukah Lights

R' Chaim took an interest in the doctor's spiritual health.

"When do you light the Chanukah candles?" R' Chaim asked the doctor.

R' Chaim lights Chanukah candles

"At 6 or 7 o'clock," the doctor answered casually, as though to say, "I do it when I can, when it's convenient for me, when I get home from work…"

But R' Chaim was not happy with this answer. "Mitzvos must be done at the right time! You should light at sunset."

R' Chaim's words had its effect. On the spot, R' Yoel called home to inform his family that he would make sure to get home early that day to light the menorah at 5 o'clock.

Sure enough, a few hours later the doctor was at home, surrounded by his family, near the Chanukah lights that had been lit with the setting of the sun — just as R' Chaim had ordered.

Then, a tragedy! A terrorist bomb had blown up a bus. Four people were killed.

A bomb? When? On which bus? The details quickly came to light. The attack had taken place on the bus that the doctor took home from work every day. The very bus that he had ridden home every day of Chanukah … except today.

Today, R' Chaim's words had hit their mark, and the doctor decided to light the menorah at its proper time. Because of R' Chaim's words, R' Yoel had returned home on an earlier bus — and been saved from the terrorist attack.

In great excitement, the doctor told R' Chaim about the miracle that had happened to him in the merit of lighting the Chanukah lights on time.

"'One who obeys the mitzvos will know no harm,'" R' Chaim quoted in reply.

It was *erev Succos*. Everyone was busy in the final hours before *Yom Tov*.

Just Before Sunset

A glance into R' Chaim Kanievsky's room aroused his family's concern. The sun would set in just an hour, and R' Chaim was asleep.

What to do? They did not like to wake him up. But they also knew he would not want to sleep outside the succah after sunset — the moment the *Yom Tov* of Succos started.

Once again, they peeked into the room. R' Chaim was still asleep.

In the succah

How stunned they were to see R' Chaim rouse from his sleep exactly at sunset; he did not sleep outside the succah on Succos for even one moment.

They had just seen the fulfillment of the *pasuk* (*Tehillim* 145:19) "*Retzon yerei'av ya'aseh* — Hashem carries out the will of those who fear Him!"

How does a person merit remembering all the Torah that one has learned: *Shas*, *poskim*, the secrets and treasures of wisdom?

The Secret of Success How does R' Chaim Kanievsky, the Prince of Torah in our own generation, manage to keep that endless store of information in his brain?

The *gadol b'Yisrael*, R' Aharon Leib Shteinman, *shlita*, explains with a *mashal*:

> To what can this be compared? To a person who has an exceptionally large store that carries thousands of items. The store owner knows exactly where each item is located and what its

R' Chaim and R' Aharon Leib

price is. How? Because this is his livelihood. The information is etched into his brain, down to the last detail.

That's how it is with R' Chaim. The Torah is his craft, and it fills his entire being. The Torah is the only topic that interests him and is important to him. Therefore, it remains in his memory as though he'd stored it safely in a box.

On different occasions, R' Shteinman has praised R' Chaim Kanievsky, saying that even decades ago people were saying that R' Chaim was a *Talmud Bavli* and *Talmud Yerushalmi* in one volume!

And that's not his only praise. Many times, R' Shteinman has used lavish expressions in praise of R' Chaim. Among them, an *olah temimah* — "a flawless offering," and a *bor sid she'einah me'abeid tipah* — "a pit lined with cement that doesn't lose a drop."

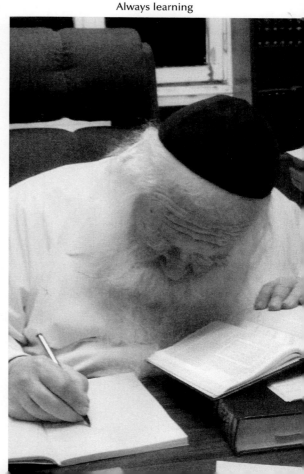

Always learning

The *Rebbetzin* Is Surprised

One morning, toward the end of the summer, the sounds of learning rose from R' Chaim Kanievsky's room. From the degree of enthusiasm, the *rebbetzin* understood that her husband, R' Chaim, was engaged in a storm of Torah study with someone. Apparently, someone had gone to his room to discuss something he was learning.

The session continued for a long time, with R' Chaim's voice speaking loudly. But when the *rebbetzin* actually looked in the room, she was in for a huge surprise. The room was empty except for her husband, sound asleep. In his sleep, he was "talking in learning" with tremendous passion.

How lucky are the grandchildren of a *tzaddik* who have the privilege of coming and going in the home of their grandfather —

Who Goes First?

listening and learning about Hashem's Torah every chance they have.

One afternoon a grandson came to see R' Chaim, who said that he'd like to tell him something about a certain *masechta* from the Gemara.

Meanwhile, another grandson entered the room with a halachic question. R' Chaim spoke to him, and then went to take his afternoon rest.

The next day, R' Chaim explained to the first grandson, "I wanted to speak with you yesterday. But because your cousin asked me a question in practical halachah, I was obligated to give him precedence!"

Torah gives strength

It was near the end of R' Yosef Shalom Elyashiv's life — the *posek hador* and father-in-law of R' Chaim Kanievsky. His anxious family saw

Weakness and Strength Together

R' Elyashiv grow so weak that he hardly had the energy to close the buttons on his coat. At the same time, they saw an amazing thing. There was no strength for fastening buttons and such things, but he continued learning Torah with his full energy. Wonder of wonders!

But R' Chaim didn't view this as an amazing thing at all. After all, he said, "Torah gives strength!"

What are the halachos of publishing a *sefer*?

There are many people who never have to deal with these laws

Halachos of Publishing

at all, or perhaps just once or twice in their lives when they have the privilege of publishing a *sefer* of Torah thought. But it is an important area for the Prince of Torah, R' Chaim Kanievsky, who has had the merit of publishing his Torah thoughts in many *sefarim*.

"Do I have to say the *berachah* of *shehecheyanu* when I put out a new *sefer*?" people ask him when they reach this milestone for the first time in their lives.

"Some people say that one should recite the *berachah*," R' Chaim tells them. "I do not make the *berachah* over a new *sefer*, but instead exempt myself by eating a new fruit. The Chazon Ish," he adds, "also did not make a *shehecheyanu* on his *sefarim* — even though he was exceedingly happy over each *sefer* — to the extent that he would say that, for him, printing each page was a joy as great as the birth of a new child."

And what about the *berachah* of *hatov u'meitiv*?

"Who says that the *sefer* is indeed good for others?" he would say. "Perhaps others will not find it useful?

"Besides, someone may come along and disprove everything that's written there, and then it will have been a *berachah l'vatalah* — a *berachah* said in vain," R' Chaim concluded.

When R' Aharon Leib Shteinman, *shlita*, was about to publish the first volume of his *sefer, Ayeles HaShachar*, he told a family member,

An Author's Fears

"I'm not afraid that someone who learns my *sefer* may disagree with an idea I wrote there. But I *am* worried that something I wrote may contradict the Gemara."

"R' Chaim Kanievsky was afraid of the same thing," his relative told him. "He was worried that something he'd written in one of his *sefarim* might contradict something in *Shas* or the *poskim*. However, as the years went by and the number of his works increased, he overcame these fears. If he found a place in *Shas* that contradicted something he wrote, he would print those words in a second edition, in the corrections at the end of the *sefer*."

"I owe So-and-so some money."
"I committed myself to helping…"

The "Debts"

"I must participate in the wedding."
"We have to visit him!"

"We have to fix the refrigerator."
"I must go to the doctor…"

Our lives are filled with various debts and responsibilities. Money debts, family responsibilities, social obligations, and much more hang around our necks.

Let us look at the debts of the *tzaddik* R' Chaim Kanievsky, *shlita*. What does he owe?

R' Chaim has a name for his uncompromising schedule of learning each day. He calls them his "*chovos*" — his debts or obligations.

These are very specific debts. Each day brings its own quota of learning: *Talmud Bavli, Talmud Yerushalmi*, Rambam, *Mishnah Berurah*, and on and on. In each area there is a fixed amount of material that can be started and finished over the course of the year.

Let's take a look at how R' Chaim uses the minutes and hours that he dedicates to Torah. Because there's learning — and there's learning!

Debts are a burden. Everyone feels a deep responsibility to pay his debts. And when debts mean promising yourself to finish a certain amount of learning each day, the commitment is just as real.

R' Chaim learned to use the word "*chovos*" about his learning from his father, the Steipler Gaon, who used that term when talking about his own regular learning commitments.

It was the summer of 2010. R' Chaim's grandson, who was living in his house at the time, saw his illustrious grandfather — despite his advanced age — finally go to sleep at a very late hour at night. Yet no more than two hours passed before R' Chaim was back "on duty" again, learning vigorously.

This pattern repeated itself day after day — after day.

"How is it possible?" the grandson asked. "How can a person get used to so little sleep?"

"I have no choice," his grandfather replied. "All through the day people come to see me, distracting me from my learning. What about my '*chovos*'? I have to learn at night to make up the time I missed

Rav Chaim "pays"
his debts every day

from my learning, at an hour when everyone is asleep and there are no interruptions."

The idea of his learning "*chovos*" — debts or obligations — is not one that R' Chaim treats lightly. When a person is burdened by debt, he is under a certain amount of stress. Anyone who sees, up close, the burden of "debt" that R' Chaim carries is aware that it creates a constant stress.

His son tells the following story:

> "For many years, I had the privilege of learning with my father, shlita. Each day, when I came to learn with him, I saw that it would not do to talk to him about anything except our regular learning, which was measured and calculated as part of his constant learning quotas.
>
> "It was clear that he was under stress to finish his daily allotment. Only when we finished learning and the daily quota was behind him was it possible to talk with him about other things."

It's a good day when a certain quota is almost reached, when the daily allotment of pages is done and the pages that are left in order to finish the *masechta* are less than another day's quota. A day like that, his family knows, is a happy one, because if there is less than a day's worth of pages left, R' Chaim will add it on to the previous day's quota. And the day that he makes a *siyum* on a *masechta* will be a day crammed with pages to learn. A day crammed with "*chovos*."

It was Rosh Chodesh Cheshvan, in the year 5771 (2011). That morning, the Kanievsky family could see that R' Chaim was in a hurry.

Making Up for Lost Time Over breakfast, a family member tried to talk to him about a number of things. It's a great privilege to live in the presence of a *gadol hador*. Every minute is precious to him. So he decided to use the time when R' Chaim was having his meal to discuss a number of important topics.

But each time he tried, R' Chaim answered, "I'm in a hurry," or "It's late," or "There's no time."

The time the *gadol* spent with people who came to see him that day was also done in a rush. R' Chaim's answers were brief, and the line moved more quickly than usual.

The family member who had earlier tried to engage R' Chaim in conversation wanted to know why R' Chaim was in such a hurry today. He asked R' Chaim whether he had a custom of learning more than usual on Rosh Chodesh. Was that why he was in such a rush?

"Davening took half an hour longer than usual today," R' Chaim answered. "There was *krias haTorah* and *Mussaf*. So now I have to make up the time to finish my quota of learning!"

The days went by, and the learning quotas marched along with them. And then came the day when R' Chaim's allotment of learning

A Great Day was doubled. On that day, he had the merit of finishing both *Talmud Bavli* and *Talmud Yerushalmi*!

These two great milestones, which had taken R' Chaim months to reach, both arrived on the same great day. When he completed *Talmud Bavli*, he drank a little wine in honor of the *siyum*. Then he finished the *Talmud Yerushalmi* and made a *siyum* on that, too. Now an unusual question cropped up. After drinking the wine for the *Talmud Bavli* and then pausing to learn *Talmud Yerushalmi*, the question was, should he make another *borei pri hagafen* or not?

Because he was in doubt about the answer, R' Chaim didn't drink wine at this *siyum*, but a little fruit juice instead.

When two people sit and learn Torah together regularly, it's natural for them to share the reasons why, on one day or another, they

How Can I Sleep? are unable to learn with full concentration. A normal day can bring all sorts of troubles and problems. Any unusual event can harm a person's alertness and powers of concentration.

"I participated in a *sheva berachos* last night"

It was time for R' Chaim Kanievsky's scheduled learning session with his son-in-law, R' Elazar Dovid Epstein, *shlita*. But today there was a change from their usual productive session. A number of times during the course of their learning, R' Chaim's eyes closed. Only after a short nap was he able to continue.

"I'm tired today," he explained to his son-in-law. "I participated in a *sheva berachos* yesterday."

This apology seemed to explain R' Chaim's tiredness, but it was only the beginning. He continued, "At the *sheva berachos*, I was asked two questions. One was whether there is a source to tell us what the ramp of the *Mizbei'ach* in the Beis HaMikdash was made of — copper or earth. The other was a question about *kilayim* (prohibited mixtures). These two questions disturbed my rest. I stayed up all night looking through the *sefarim* searching for answers."

The less-than-fully-alert learning session turned into an important lesson in *mussar*.

What does an elderly Jew do on his return from a *simchah* late at night? What does an aged man do when he has two demanding questions niggling at his brain?

How could he ignore the questions and simply go to sleep? He couldn't! He had to toil and seek until he found a good answer!

The personality of the *sandak* at a bris milah has an effect on the spiritual future of the baby having the bris. That's why we seek

A Different Kind of Wealth to have someone who has the stature to be a proper *sandak*. It's no surprise, then, that R' Chaim Kanievsky is asked to serve as a *sandak* nearly every day.

Serving as a *sandak* is a great merit, and for many years R' Chaim would travel all over the country for this purpose. Apart from the merit of the mitzvah, being a *sandak* is considered a *segulah* for becoming wealthy. But the truth is that even though R' Chaim was rich in the honor of being a *sandak*, he was not rich in money.

"Where is the wealth that one is supposed to get for being a *sandak*?" someone once asked him. "After all, Rebbe serves as a *sandak* nearly every day!"

R' Chaim replied that his father, the Steipler Gaon, also served as *sandak* for a great many bris milah ceremonies and he was not

The Steipler at a bris

wealthy in cash, either. He would say that his wealth was in the *sefarim* he wrote.

"And so it is with me," R' Chaim said. Then he added, "And the grandchildren that are born each year — are they not riches? Grandchildren are the greatest wealth!"

"Can the Rav tell me," asked R' Eliyahu Mann, a *meshamesh* of R' Chaim Kanievsky's, "why the Rav agrees to serve as *sandak* at bris

The Secret of Time

after bris? True, it's a big mitzvah. But doesn't it say, *Talmud Torah keneged kulam* — that learning Torah is worth more than all other mitzvos?"

R' Chaim said, "My father-in-law, R' Elyashiv, *zt"l*, once asked me the same question. Why do I go to so many bris milahs? I answered that that's what I saw from my *rebbeim*. The Chazon Ish never refused to serve as *sandak* at a bris. Once, he traveled all the way to Komemiyus on roundabout roads. The round trip from Bnei Brak to Komemiyus and back took most of the day!

"My father, the Steipler, was the same. He, too, never refused to serve as *sandak*. We know what the Chasam Sofer said: one who spends a long time davening will have long years of life. We can understand from this that a person who devotes extra time to his *tefillah* will not lose time, Heaven forbid; on the contrary, he will *gain* time. It seems that this is true of all the mitzvos. Through doing a mitzvah, one's years are lengthened. He will receive extra time!"

"I've come to ask the Rav to be the *sandak* at my son's bris," said the father of a new baby boy.

What Happened to the Car?

When R' Chaim Kanievsky gave his consent, the father offered to send a car to pick him up. He had an idea of whom to send for this privilege. He knew a man, a *ba'al teshuvah*, who would be overjoyed to drive R' Chaim Kanievsky to the bris.

On the day of the bris, at the appointed hour, the car waited outside the Kanievsky home. The excited driver eagerly awaited the

Only in a
car that is
"pure"

moment when the Prince of Torah would get into his car and he'd have the privilege of driving him.

R' Chaim emerged from the house and started walking toward the car. The driver, who had been standing respectfully outside the car, got in and started the engine.

That is, he *tried* to start it. Tried and failed.

He tried again. Maybe he was just too excited and wasn't doing it right.

He tried this way and that, but the car refused to budge. With no choice, R' Chaim went to the bris in a different car.

It was later that the reason for the first car's trouble came to light.

The car had been bought by the *ba'al teshuvah's* father using money earned from *ribbis* — interest — which is forbidden in the Torah. Heaven had protected R' Chaim from deriving the slightest benefit from the forbidden *ribbis*.

R' Chaim is always extremely careful to avoid even the tiniest suspicious of *ribbis*. He makes sure to keep his money only in a bank that does not have any problems with the *issur* of taking interest.

And because he'd worked hard to stay far away from *ribbis* all of his life, he was protected from riding in the car that was paid for with money from *ribbis*!

It was R' Chaim's practice — as it had been his father's before him — to visit each grandchild who had married and set up a home

"Shmattes" in the Bookcase

of his own. These visits brought the young couple great joy.

It was the beginning of the winter, and the newly married grandson and his wife eagerly awaited the promised visit.

Finally, it came to be. The door opened, and the Prince of Torah, R' Chaim Kanievsky, walked inside. The first thing he passed through was a long hall.

R' Chaim's reaction to the sight of that hall? "You'll have a hard time checking for *chametz*." To him, a large house was a source of possible problems in fulfilling the mitzvah to get rid of *chametz* properly and other mitzvos.

When they entered the room, R' Chaim's eyes went to the breakfront. Silver ornaments gleamed on its shelves.

The joy of simplicity

"What is that box with all the *shmattes* inside?" he asked, gesturing at the breakfront. "When you have some more *sefarim*, take out the *shmattes* and put *sefarim* in!"

His grandson accepted the brief lesson, in which he'd learned some new things about owning possessions in this world:

A long hall = extra work.

A breakfront = a box.

Silver ornaments = *shmattes*.

it was a memorable visit – and a lesson well learned.

America was having an unusually hard winter. News of a big storm reached the shores of Eretz Yisrael.

The Right Size for a House

"Oh no," everyone said in distress. "The storm is creating so much destruction! Tall buildings have collapsed in the wind. Skyscrapers have fallen down like a house of cards. What a pity. So much property has been lost."

R' Chaim's home

The sad news reached R' Chaim Kanievsky as well. But while the others were upset about the end of the story, they discovered that R' Chaim was disturbed by the beginning of it.

"If there are such tall buildings over there in America, how do they do *bedikas chametz*?"

R' Chaim himself takes a great deal of time over *bedikas chametz* and invests a great deal of energy in the mitzvah. *Bedikas chametz*, therefore, is the yardstick by which he defines the ideal house size!

A man came to see the *posek hador*, R' Yosef Shalom Elyashiv, with a question. As he entered the room, he saw that R' Elyashiv was

A Lesson in Humility

so completely immersed in what he was learning that he did not even notice the man's arrival.

The man waited for five minutes, staring and marveling. As he stood there, he noticed that the *sefer* R' Elyashiv was learning was that of R' Elyashiv's son-in-law, R' Chaim Kanievsky: *Derech Emunah*.

Why not tell R' Chaim about this? the man asked himself.

And so he did.

When R' Chaim heard that his father-in-law had been so completely absorbed in his *sefer*, he said humbly, "He probably saw a favorable comment about the *sefer*."

R' Chaim saw no reason to consider this news a compliment to him. In his great humility, he though the exact opposite: If R' Elyashiv had been reading his work with such intense concentration, he probably had some sort of comment to make on what was written there.

The man was confused. The incident he had just related would have made anyone else extremely happy. But R' Chaim, in his modesty, had changed the picture from one extreme to the other.

It was a good thing he'd taken the trouble to come here, the man thought. At the father-in-law's house he had witnessed unparalleled concentration in learning and, at the son-in-law's, he had just received a short but powerful lesson in humility.

"Doctor, I'm in a lot of pain."

"I have no appetite."

The Patient Speaks

"I'm so dizzy!"

"It's hard for me to walk."

"I feel queasy."

Doctors are used to hearing symptoms like these. This has become routine in any clinic or hospital.

Dr. Hart, a hospital physician, was as used to hearing these kinds of complaints as any other doctor. And then he met a very different kind of patient.

It was in the winter of 2013. R' Chaim Kanievsky was rushed to the hospital, where he was diagnosed as having a broken bone.

R' Chaim did not complain to the doctor about the pain he was in. He did not mention the swelling or the restriction in his ability to move. Instead, he shared a concern: "Chazal say that in the future the *bechorim* — firstborn sons — will work in the Beis HaMikdash. I am a *bechor*." He was troubled. "Who knows if this broken bone won't disqualify me for the *avodah* in the Beis HaMikdash?"

The doctor was stunned to hear what this elderly Jew was worried about while suffering the pain of a broken bone.

R' Chaim didn't mind the pain. What concerned him was whether his injury might be considered a blemish that would disqualify him from work in the future Beis HaMikdash.

R' Chaim Kanievsky needed an operation to remove cataracts from his eyes — so decreed the doctors. Cataract operations are

Fresh Eyes

common and widespread among the elderly population.

When the operation was over, the doctor wanted to check the condition of R' Chaim's eye. Was the operation a success?

He handed R' Chaim a newspaper, but R' Chaim was not comfortable with this reading material, even though it was a religious newspaper. Putting down the paper, he said, "I have received a new eye. The first thing I should read with it is the Gemara!"

At a gathering, with other *gedolim*

R' Chaim Kanievsky receives a great many invitations, some of them verbal and others in writing.

Why Did He Stay?   Yeshivos, institutions, organizations — who does not want R' Chaim to enhance their event with his sparkling *divrei Torah*? Whether they are laying a cornerstone for a new building or celebrating a *hachnasas sefer Torah*, whether it is assemblies and memorials or eulogies and public *siyums*, everyone wants the honor of having R' Chaim attend. Of course, it's impossible to participate in all of them. But it's also impossible to stay away from them all. Here and there, when necessary, R' Chaim attends such events for a short time.

One day, at such an event, the men in charge were surprised to see R' Chaim grace the hall for a fairly lengthy time — longer than usual for him. Why had they merited this good fortune? Why, his companions asked, had R' Chaim decided to remain at this event longer than usual?

R' Chaim explained: Once the speeches started, he felt that he couldn't leave. If he left between one speech and the next, people might think that he wasn't interested in hearing the words of the next speaker. R' Chaim would never dream of embarrassing someone that way. So he remained for a longer time than he'd originally intended.

R' Chaim Kanievsky has a custom of giving his granddaughters a siddur when they reach the age of bas mitzvah.

No Cause for Jealousy When his son's second daughter turned 12, R' Chaim asked her father to look at the siddur that he had given the older daughter. He explained, "I want to copy the *berachah* I wrote there for your older daughter, to make sure I don't write anything less for the second one than I wrote to the first — or anything more. I do not want to cause jealousy between them."

Foundation Stones It was *motza'ei Shabbos*, 2010, the night when R' Chaim Kanievsky's sister, Rebbetzin Berman, passed from this world. The funeral was held in the middle of the night. It was close to 2 a.m. by the time the mourners returned home after laying her to rest. They davened *Ma'ariv*. R' Chaim recited "*V'Yitein Lecha*" word for word, and then went to eat a meal for *melaveh malkah*.

It was his custom to have a meat meal for *melaveh malkah* each week. That night, although it was hard for him to eat a bite, he rose above his natural feelings and ate a little meat.

It was past 2 o'clock when the meal was done. R' Chaim went to sleep. Two hours later, just after 4 a.m., he got up, took out his Mishnah, and sat down to learn those *sefarim* that one is permitted to learn during the week of mourning.

The routines of life continued in their accustomed ways, with Torah study and scrupulousness in halachah serving as the foundation stones for any situation.

Chol HaMo'ed Succos, 5772 (2011). The happiness of *Yom Tov* was tragically disrupted when Rebbetzin Batsheva Kanievsky, wife of

The Most Decisive Question

the Prince of Torah, R' Chaim Kanievsky, was unexpectedly taken from this world.

The bitter sorrow in that great house did not change the essence of life in the Kanievsky home. Torah study remained its central focus, even in the difficult days before the *shivah*, which was postponed because of *Yom Tov* until *motza'ei Simchas Torah*.

R' Chaim Kanievsky undertook to learn the laws of *aveilus* down to the last detail. For him, the most important question of all was this: was he permitted to learn Torah on Chol HaMo'ed, before the *shivah* started?

This was the paramount question, and one that would decide the nature of those difficult days for him.

Rebbetzin Batsheva Kanievsky, *a"h*, the wife of R' Chaim Kanievsky, passed away very suddenly on Shabbos, Chol HaMo'ed Succos. It was

Unwavering

impressive to see the way R' Chaim's mind controlled his emotions, and how even during those very difficult moments he pushed aside his feelings for the sanctity of the Shabbos.

He didn't react at all. He merely sat alone and silent out of honor for the Shabbos. Only on *motza'ei Shabbos* did he finally allow himself to weep.

The official week of mourning began the moment *Yom Tov* ended. On Isru Chag, which fell out on a Friday, the family was restless and agitated in the wake of the unexpected tragedy. For a minute they thought R' Chaim felt the same way. Usually, when he wanted to summon one of his relatives, he would ring a bell. Today, however, he called out to them. Apparently, the tragedy had influenced his habits.

But when they asked him why he hadn't used the bell, they discovered that even now, in this very difficult time, everything R' Chaim did was as thought out as always.

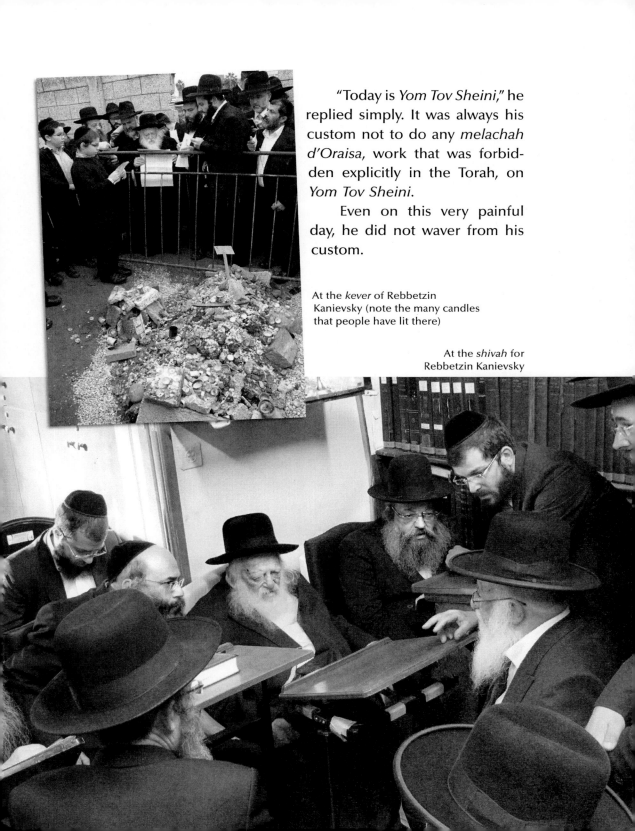

"Today is *Yom Tov Sheini*," he replied simply. It was always his custom not to do any *melachah d'Oraisa*, work that was forbidden explicitly in the Torah, on *Yom Tov Sheini*.

Even on this very painful day, he did not waver from his custom.

At the *kever* of Rebbetzin Kanievsky (note the many candles that people have lit there)

At the *shivah* for Rebbetzin Kanievsky

R' Gedalia Honigsberg, *shlita*, a grandson of both R' Aharon Leib Shteinman, *shlita*, and R' Chaim Kanievsky, *shlita*, is a frequent visitor at the homes of both of his illustrious grandfathers.

Two Big Luminaries He has ample opportunity to see how these two spiritual giants honor and appreciate each other.

"You have to ask R' Chaim Kanievsky that question," R' Aharon Leib Shteinman frequently remarks.

"This question has to be answered by R' Aharon Leib Shteinman," R' Chaim often declares.

Not only questions are sent back and forth between them, but also requests to daven for someone. In fact, the two *gedolim* daven for each other regularly.

Very often, R' Chaim will ask, "How is R' Aharon Leib?" And then he adds, "Hashem should help him and give him strength. He needs to be healthy. He is the leader of *Klal Yisrael*, and we need him!"

R' Chaim has often said that our whole generation depends on R' Aharon Leib Shteinman, *shlita*, as it says in *Sefer Chassidim* that there are always a few individuals on whose shoulders the generation rests.

Rav Aharon Leib Shteinman

Similarly, R' Shteinman says of R' Chaim, "The generation rests on the Prince of Torah, HaGaon R' Chaim Kanievsky, *shlita*!"

According to R' Chaim Kanievsky, *shechalak meichachmaso lirei'av,*

A *Berachah* for the Wise "Who has apportioned of His knowledge to those who fear Him," is a *berachah* that one recites when in the presence of someone who is considered a *gadol hador* and outstanding in Torah study.

Baking matzahs

In his opinion, he felt that this *berachah* should be recited when one saw R' Shach, *zt"l*, as well as R' Elyashiv, *zt"l*. He also instructs people to say this *berachah* when they see R' Aharon Leib Shteinman, *shlita*.

It was matzah-baking time. The atmosphere was tense. Everyone was absorbed in making sure the matzos came out perfectly. Every

Soothing Words   person was involved in his task. They called out to each other, urging each other to hurry. It was a fight to beat the clock.

Another Jew ran around as well. His job was not connected to baking matzos. He had a different job.

He was a professional photographer. Hearing that R' Chaim Kanievsky would be baking matzos here today, he had come to take pictures.

He was not satisfied with just one picture. He wanted to take as many pictures as possible throughout the whole baking process. He stood here and he stood there. One of the men in charge kept bumping into him and finally lost his temper.

Writing in a *sefer Torah*

"This is disturbing us!" he told the photographer. "This is not the time to take pictures!"

As you can imagine, the photographer felt very upset. When the baking was done, R' Chaim Kanievsky went over to the photographer and offered some comforting words.

"Don't worry about the shouting," he said pleasantly. "Sometimes people get too angry."

Now the photographer was able to leave in a much better frame of mind. He had the pictures he wanted, and he also had R' Chaim's soothing words, which stayed with him for a long, long time.

We all know an important lesson that Chazal have taught us: *Derech eretz kadmah laTorah* — *derech eretz* comes before Torah. For

A New Sefer Torah
R' Chaim Kanievsky, *derech eretz* also comes before writing a *sefer Torah*.

R' Chaim is often asked to write a letter in a new *sefer Torah*. Picture the scene. The house where the *sefer Torah* has just been completed bustles with noise. People mill about as the final preparations are made for the *seudah* to follow. The man donating the *sefer Torah* is filled with joy as everyone goes over to him and shakes his hand.

It sometimes happens that the *sofer*, who toiled so long and hard to write that *sefer Torah*, is not treated as he deserves at this exalted moment. He gave his best to produce a beautiful and holy *sefer Torah*. Isn't this *his* celebration, too?

Whenever R' Chaim is invited to such ceremonies to write one of the last letters in the *sefer Torah*, he is always careful to ask, "Who wrote this *sefer Torah*? Where is the *sofer*?"

Then the *sofer*, who may have been standing on the sidelines, has the privilege of receiving R' Chaim's praise. "Beautiful writing!" R' Chaim will say warmly. And the *sofer* glows, knowing those two simple words are a fair exchange for all his long, hard work.

And all the people present at the celebration have the privilege of watching a short lesson in *mussar* — a lesson in very few words. They learn that treating another person kindly is something that we must always try to do, no matter when and where we are.

It was the spring of 5773 (2013). The new *mikveh* that had been built in Bnei Brak was ready. Everything was in place except for the

Winter in Spring

main thing: rain to fill it up.

Community activists wondered, How could they fill the pit? The winter months were behind them, and Pesach had already come and gone. In Eretz Yisrael, the amount of rain needed to fill a *mikveh* falls only in the winter months. Even if there might be a sprinkle or two in the spring, it wouldn't be enough.

The new mikveh was very much needed, but it didn't seem possible that they could use it in the next few months. It looked like the *mikveh* would have to stand empty and unused for the next seven months. What a pity!

R' Chaim with R' Avraham Rubinstein, former mayor of Bnei Brak

In light of the situation, the head of the municipality, R' Avraham Rubinstein, *shlita*, decided to ask R' Chaim Kanievsky, for a *berachah*.

"The *mikveh* that was just built in Shikun Gimmel needs rainwater," R' Rubinstein said.

R' Chaim gave him a *berachah* that rain would fall and fill the new *mikveh*.

The residents of Bnei Brak were astonished at the weather. Suddenly it was winter all over again! First it got cold, and then the rain started falling nonstop.

Strange — very strange. Rain? Such cold weather, and such strong rain, just like the middle of the winter.

"It's cold today," R' Chaim's family told him. "The Rav should wear a sweater,"

"A sweater?" he asked. "Why a sweater? We're already davening *Morid hatal*!" What he meant was — it's springtime!

"They're saying that the Rav gave a *berachah* that rain should fall for the *mikveh*."

"Find out if the reservoir of water for the *mikveh* is full of rain-water, so summer can come," R' Chaim said. He wanted to know if the necessary quantity of water had fallen for the *mikveh*.

"No, it still needs more water," the community activists said.

"Let all the necessary water fill the *mikveh*," R' Chaim blessed. Indeed, the heavy rain continued to fall for a number of days. Amazing!

Several times during those days, R' Chaim mentioned that the rain was falling in order to fill the *mikveh*. The head of the municipality kept checking the water level and reporting back to R' Chaim.

On *erev Shabbos, Parashas Acharei Mos–Kedoshim*, he sent word to R' Chaim that 150 liters of water were still missing.

"*Im yirtzeh Hashem*," R' Chaim replied. If it's Hashem's will...

That Shabbos, the tenth day of Iyar, a very heavy rain fell. The old-timers of Bnei Brak didn't remember such a rainy day on the tenth day of the month of Iyar in their lives. That Shabbos, as well, R' Chaim said that the rain was falling in the merit of the mitzvah of *mikveh*.

One day, one of R' Chaim's grandsons was discussing a certain topic in *Maseches Avodah Zarah* with him. R' Chaim asked the boy,

If You Really Want It

"Haven't you learned *Maseches Avodah Zarah*?"

"Not yet," the grandson replied.

"At your age," R' Chaim said, "one should already be familiar with all of *Shas*. If I had the strength, I'd learn with you myself."

Then he added, "When I was young, I would learn all of *Shas* every year, with *Tosafos*. I didn't learn it in great depth, but I reviewed all the topics. In general, it's worthwhile to learn all of *Shas* at a young age, even if you don't understand it so well, so that the subject matter will not be unfamiliar to you. In the earlier cycles, I learned it more in depth, and in my later years I learned only with *Tosafos*. It's not difficult, if you really want it!"

Sefarim,
everywhere

Another time, he
once told one of his descendants, "When I was a *bachur* in
yeshivah, I completed *Maseches Yevamos*
four times."

An old *chavrusa* of R' Chaim's had a look at R' Chaim's Gemara
Yevamos from their yeshivah days. On the inside cover was a list that
testified to all the times that R' Chaim had reviewed the *masechta*:
"I started on 1 Cheshvan..." "I started on 1 Kislev..." "1 Teves..." "1
Shevat..."

The walls of the Kanievsky home are lined with bookcases. There
are shelves in every possible corner, each one containing *sifrei kodesh*

Respecting Sefarim

from which R' Chaim learns day and night.
Even though there are *sefarim* just about everywhere, R' Chaim is always careful not to sit with his
back to the *sefarim*! When he goes to other people's homes for a
bris milah, he makes sure to sit in such a way that the bookcase is

not behind his back, because it is not respectful to *sefarim* to sit that way!

When he enters a *beis midrash* or private home and sees *sefarim* that are not placed in a respectful way, he will personally hurry over and straighten them out without delay.

On *motza'ei Shabbos, Parashas Vayikra* 2013, a large gathering was held to strengthen *bnei yeshivah*. The organizers came and asked

Wrong Address
R' Chaim Kanievsky to deliver a speech at the gathering.

"Thirty thousand *bachurim* are waiting for the Rav," the organizers told him.

But R' Chaim answered simply, "It can't be. You must have the wrong address."

On another occasion, one of R' Chaim's grandsons related the following:

"Hashem gave me the *zechus* of being with R' Chaim every morning. When Purim came, though, things got changed around. Instead of coming in the morning, I went there on *motza'ei Purim*.

"When I came in, I said, 'I didn't have the *zechus* of coming this morning. *Shamayim* gave me the *zechus* of coming at night instead.'

"My grandfather shrugged this off, as if to say it was nothing special.

"But I kept talking about the great privilege it was to be with him. Hearing me, R' Chaim said, 'If you're talking that way, you must have drunk some wine.'"

Another time, R' Chaim said that his custom when saying *Krias Shema* was to say *Kel melech ne'eman*, because sometimes he didn't hear the chazzan and sometimes he finished Shema after the chazzan. These words are said when a person is not davening Shema with a *minyan*.

"How is it possible that you finish Shema after the chazzan? The shul waits for you!" someone asked.

"What do you mean, they wait for me?" R' Chaim asked with complete simplicity, incredulous that everyone would wait for him to finish davening. "How would they know when I'm finished?"

Then he added, "My father, the Steipler, also used to say *Kel melech ne'eman*."

And the listener knew that R' Chaim's humility was inherited from a holy source.

The Best Comfort

It was the last days of the year 5774 — September 2013. The death of R' Chaim Kanievsky's daughter, Rebbetzin Chana Shteinman, a"h, brought much pain and anguish. It also brought seven days without his regular learning to the bereaved father, during the *shivah*.

There are certain subjects that may be learned during mourning. But his usual quota of studies in *Talmud Bavli*, *Talmud Yerushalmi*, and all the rest — for this week, Rav Chaim could not complete his "*chovos*."

On the seventh morning, the family followed the custom of going to visit the new grave in the cemetery. On their return, R' Chaim — again, as per custom — ate a bit of breakfast. Immediately after finishing his short meal, he went looking for his Gemara — specifically, *Maseches Gittin*, the place he was up to in his learning before the *shivah* started.

His beloved learning

He opened up his beloved Gemara, and the learning schedule began. Hour after hour after hour.

The morning passed in a flash. It was time for *Minchah*. *Baruch Hashem*, he had succeeded in finishing his quota in *Gittin* for all the seven days of mourning. In fact, by *Minchah* time he had managed to complete *all* of *Maseches Gittin*!

After davening, R' Chaim asked for a *Yerushalmi Gittin* to be brought to him. He began in the place where he'd left off before the *shivah* and went on until he finished *Gittin* in the *Talmud Yerushalmi* as well.

And so he continued. For ten consecutive hours, he continued his learning schedule and "obligations," until he'd covered all the material that he would have covered during the seven days of mourning.

Near sunset, R' Chaim got up and told his family, "*Baruch Hashem*, I've managed to complete what was missing in my regular learning. Now I can go on with my usual schedule."

Only then did he lie down for a little rest.

His family had merited seeing, with their own eyes, the fulfillment of the verse *Had not your Torah been my preoccupation, then I would have perished in my affliction* (*Tehillim* 119:92).

Only the Torah had the power to heal a heart in pain after losing a loved one and a body frail from a week of deep mourning, especially at such an advanced age. R' Chaim had overcome any weakness he might have felt and thrown himself back into the business of learning Torah.

In the course of his daily learning, R' Chaim picked up a *Maseches Avodah Zarah*, followed by *Maseches Horayos* and several smaller

Who Wants to See Eliyahu HaNavi?

tractates, such as *Avos*, *Avos D'Rabbi Nassan*, and *Maseches Sofrim*. When he reached *Maseches Kallah Rabbasi*, he learned with deep absorption for several hours.

Suddenly, he lifted his eyes and asked his grandson, "Are you interested in seeing Eliyahu HaNavi?"

"Of course!" the grandson answered in amazement. Who wouldn't be?

"Then see what it says here." R' Chaim pointed to a line in *Maseches Kallah Rabbasi*. "R' Abba Eliyahu said, 'The Torah is well understood only by a person who is not overly strict and demanding of others. I [Eliyahu], too, reveal myself only to those who are not too strict with others. Happy is the person who meets him and sits with him, for he is assured that he is a *ben Olam HaBa*!'"

R' Chaim repeated these words out loud, with emotion. "Here is an idea for how to merit seeing Eliyahu — not to be overly demanding and to behave pleasantly with other people!"

Mazel tov! Mazel tov! Everybody congratulated the *bachur* on his engagement. May he establish an everlasting home! May all the

Always Be Prepared

preparations for his new life go smoothly, with Heaven's help!

The next weeks were very busy ones. There were things to arrange and items to buy. There was a stack of wedding invitations to send. On top of all that, the *chasan* realized that he

Maybe someone will ask to hear your *derashah*..."

would also have to prepare a *derashah* — a speech. In his family, there was a custom for a *chasan* to speak at his wedding.

But the *chasan* knew that this custom did not exist at other weddings. In that case, why should he take the trouble? *I have so much to arrange,* he thought. *I only*

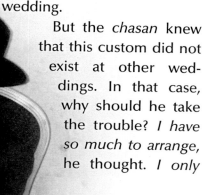

hope I manage to get everything done in time! If they won't ask me to speak at the wedding anyway, it would be a pity to take the time to prepare a derashah.

So thought R' Chaim Kanievsky's grandson. "Why should I prepare a *derashah*," he asked his grandfather, "when in the end I probably won't be asked to say it?"

But his grandfather did not agree. "Prepare a *derashah*!" he advised. "One must always be prepared. You don't know who will be seated beside you at the table. Maybe you won't speak in public. But maybe someone next to you will ask to hear your *derashah*. That's what happened at my own wedding.

"When I got married," he continued, "sitting next to me at the table was R' Yitzchak Meir Pachiner, the son-in-law of R' Isser Zalman Meltzer."

R' Pachiner was an important *dayan*, someone to be respected both for his age and wisdom.

"'I'd like to hear your *derashah*,' he told me.

"I started to say the *derashah*, thinking that the elderly *dayan* would not take the time to listen for more than a few minutes. Also, the commotion all around us didn't make it easy to concentrate. But R' Yitzchak Meir Pachiner listened to the entire *derashah*, from beginning to end.

"So, you see," R' Chaim concluded, "it's always best to be prepared!"

Each year, on Succos, R' Chaim Kanievsky has the custom of traveling up to Yerushalayim.

Only After Sunset   He makes a point of going to the Kosel HaMa'aravi after the sun has set, because he is concerned that those in the city are obligated by the Torah to take the *arba'ah minim*.

"Who knows if my *arba'ah minim* are *mehudar* enough to let me fulfill my obligation in the mitzvah?"

At the Kosel

In order not to enter into this possible doubt on a Torah law, R' Chaim is careful to arrive at the Kosel at an hour when one does not have to carry the *arba'ah minim*.

Each year, Jews at the Kosel HaMa'aravi receive a reminder from this great man of halachah, for whom every single letter in the Torah shines like a light: in every action that we do, at any time of the day or night, we must always consider the halachic aspect!

Those close to R' Chaim Kanievsky speak about how careful he was with halachah even when he was sick and confined to a hospital bed.

A Timeless Message

"Every move he made was according to halachah, down to the last detail. Even when he was feeling very weak, his family saw him keep every part of halachah," they related.

"The minute it was time to put on tefillin, he hurried to put on his tefillin and daven *k'vasikin* (starting very early in the morning, before sunrise). And when it was time for *Minchah*, he davened immediately, despite his great weakness."

"One time," one relative related, "when he was feeling especially weak, he was given a pill that he had to take right away. But before he swallowed it, he asked, 'Did they check the kashrus of this medicine?'

"After hearing the answer, he asked another question: 'Is it bitter, so that there's no need to make a *berachah* on it, or sweet, and thus requiring a *berachah*?'"

At all times, in every place, a Jew remembers the halachah. That is the constant message and the timeless lesson of R' Chaim Kanievsky, the Prince of Torah.

Rav Chaim, the Prince of Torah